Integrated Spelling

GRADE 3

Harcourt Brace & Company

Orlando Atlanta Austin Boston San Francisco Chicago Dallas New York Toronto London

Copyright © by Harcourt Brace & Company

All rights reserved. No part of this publication may be reproduced or transmitted in any form or by any means, electronic or mechanical, including photocopy, recording, or any information storage and retrieval system, without permission in writing from the publisher.

Permission is hereby granted to individual teachers using the corresponding student's textbook or kit as the major vehicle for regular classroom instruction to photocopy complete pages from this publication in classroom quantities for instructional use and not for resale.

Duplication of this work other than by individual classroom teachers under the conditions specified above requires a license. To order a license to duplicate this work in greater than classroom quantities, contact Customer Service, Harcourt Brace & Company, 6277 Sea Harbor Drive, Orlando, Florida 32887-6777. Telephone: 1-800-225-5425. Fax: 1-800-874-6418 or 407-352-3442.

HARCOURT BRACE and Quill Design is a registered trademark of Harcourt Brace & Company

Printed in the United States of America

ISBN 0-15-310825-8

1 2 3 4 5 6 7 8 9 10   054   2001 2000 99 98

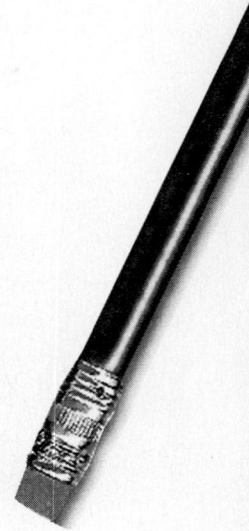

Contents

Making Your Spelling Log 5
Study Steps to Learn a Word 8

UNIT 1

LESSON	1	Words with Short *a* and Short *e* 10
LESSON	2	Words with Short *i*, Short *o*, and Short *u* 14
LESSON	3	Words with Long *i* and Long *o* 18
LESSON	4	Words with Long *a* and Long *e* 22
LESSON	5	Consonant Clusters 26
LESSON	6	**Review** 30

UNIT 2

LESSON	7	Words with *kn*, *wr*, *gh*, and *ph* 34
LESSON	8	Words with *sh*, *ch*, and *wh* 38
LESSON	9	Words Like *zoo* and *good* 42
LESSON	10	Words Like *small* 46
LESSON	11	Words with *-er* and *-est* 50
LESSON	12	**Review** 54

UNIT 3

LESSON	13	Words Like *joy* and *down* 58
LESSON	14	Words Like *yard* and *air* 62
LESSON	15	Words Like *your* 66
LESSON	16	Homophones 70
LESSON	17	Calendar Words 74
LESSON	18	**Review** 78

Integrated Spelling

UNIT 4

LESSON 19	Words Like *her*	82
LESSON 20	Words That End with *-ed* and *-ing*	86
LESSON 21	Words Like *ago* and *begin*	90
LESSON 22	Contractions and Possessives	94
LESSON 23	More Possessives	98
LESSON 24	**Review**	102

UNIT 5

LESSON 25	Changing *y* to *i*	106
LESSON 26	Words Like *dinner*	110
LESSON 27	Words with Suffixes	114
LESSON 28	Words That End Like *happy*	118
LESSON 29	Compound Words	122
LESSON 30	Suffix: *-y*	126
LESSON 31	**Review**	130

UNIT 6

LESSON 32	Words That End Like *never*	134
LESSON 33	Words That End Like *little*	138
LESSON 34	Words That End Like *seven*	142
LESSON 35	Words Like *alive* and *beneath*	146
LESSON 36	**Review**	150

Spelling Table 154
Spelling Dictionary 156
The Writing Process 178
    Proofreading Checklist 179
Spelling Strategies 180
Spelling Log 182

Making Your Spelling Log

This book gives you a place to keep a word list of your own. It's called a **SPELLING LOG**!

If you need some **IDEAS** for creating your list, just look at what I usually do!

While I read, I look for words that I think are **INTERESTING.** I listen for **NEW WORDS** used by people on radio and television.

I include words that I need to use when I **WRITE,** especially words that are hard for me to spell.

Before I write a word in my Spelling Log, I check the spelling. I look up the word in a **DICTIONARY** or a **THESAURUS,** or I ask for help.

To help me understand and remember the meaning of my word, I write a **DEFINITION,** a **SYNONYM,** or an **ANTONYM.** I also use my word in a sentence.

Making Your Spelling Log

Here's how you use it!

THE SPELLING LOG SECTION of this book is just for you. It's your own list of words that you want to remember. Your Spelling Log has three parts. Here's how to use each part.

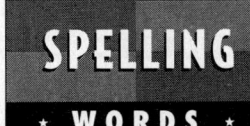

Spelling Words to Study

This is where you'll list words from each lesson that you need to study. Include words you misspell on the pretest and any other words you aren't sure you can always spell correctly.

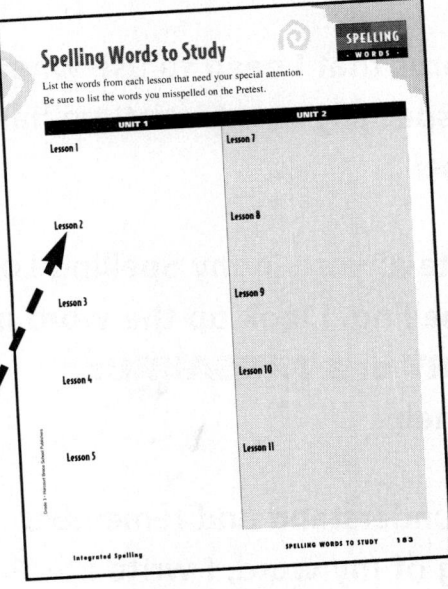

This handy list makes it easy for me to study the words I need to learn!

I'll write a clue beside each word to help me remember it.

WordShop WORDS

Vocabulary WordShop Words

These pages are for listing the WordShop Words from each lesson. Group the words any way you like, and write them on the pages where you think they belong. You'll find pages for language, social studies and science, and art and music.

Your Own WORDS

My Own Word Collection

You choose the words to list on these pages. Include new words, interesting words, and any other words you want to remember. You decide how to group them, too!

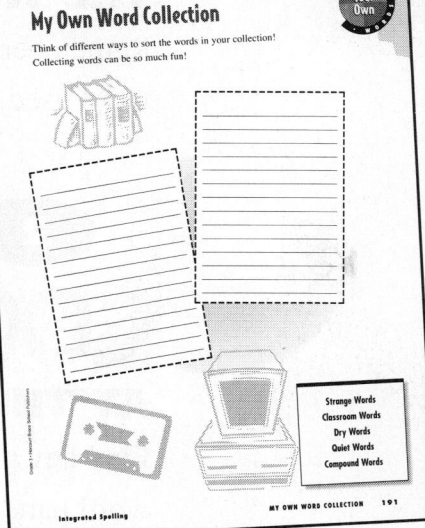

Hints may help you think of categories for your words!

Integrated Spelling — MAKING YOUR SPELLING LOG

Study Steps to Learn a Word

Check out these steps.

1 SAY THE WORD.

Remember when you have heard the word used. Think about what it means.

2 LOOK AT THE WORD.

Find any prefixes, suffixes, or other word parts you know. Think of another word that is related in meaning and spelling. Try to picture the word in your mind.

3 SPELL
THE WORD TO YOURSELF.
Think about the way each sound is spelled. Notice any unusual spelling.

4 WRITE
THE WORD WHILE YOU ARE LOOKING AT IT.
Check the way you have formed your letters. If you have not written the word clearly or correctly, write it again.

5 CHECK
WHAT YOU HAVE LEARNED.
Cover the word and write it. If you have not spelled the word correctly, practice these steps until you can write it correctly every time.

SPELLING WORDS

1. best
2. nap
3. end
4. act
5. tell
6. went
7. left
8. fat
9. head
10. next
11. hand
12. bread

Look for other words with the short *a* and short *e* sounds to add to the lists. You can find *add* or *tens* in your math book. If you read a book about music, you might see *staff* or *rest*.

13. _____
14. _____
15. _____

Words with Short *a* and Short *e*

Each Spelling Word has the short *a* or the short *e* sound. Look at the letters that spell those sounds.

Sort the Spelling Words in a way that will help you remember them. Two example words are given.

short a
cat

short e
bed

▶ The short *a* sound can be spelled *a*.
▶ The short *e* sound can be spelled *e* or *ea*.

Name _____

Strategy Workshop

PROOFREADING: Checking Spelling When you proofread, look for words that may be misspelled. Circle words that do not look right. Then check the spelling in a dictionary.

Which words do not look right to you? In each row, circle the words that have spelling errors. Check the spelling in the Spelling Dictionary, and then write the correct spelling for each word.

✓ 1. (aact)   nap   ✓ 2. (hed)   best
  3. went   ✓(hend)   ✓ 4. bread (faht)
  5. (eind)   tell   ✓ 6. (leeft) next

7–11. Proofread the postcard. Circle the five words that do not look right. Check the spelling, and then write the correct spelling.

1. act
2. hand
3. left
4. head
5. fat
6. end

Dear Molly,
 My granny is the (bast) cook! We (wint) berry picking, and she made pies. She even bakes her own (brad). Naxt to her stove is a big cooling rack for all her goodies. Tel everyone at home that I say "Hi"!
 Your best friend,
 Liza

Molly Gordon
760 Lowell Street
Livingston, MA 02234

7. best
8. went
9. bread
10. _____
11. _____

FUN WITH WORDS Write a Spelling Word to complete the riddle.

What do you call a kitten's snooze?

12. A cat's ____!

12. _____

Integrated Spelling   LESSON 1   11

Name _____

Assignment WORDS

story
due
library
homework

SPELLING LOG Think about how you might use these words in your writing, and add them to your Spelling Log.

1. _____
2. _____
3. _____
4. _____

5. _____
6. _____
7. _____
8. _____
9. _____
10. _____

Vocabulary WordShop

Use the Assignment Words to complete the daily calendar.

Monday	Do my _1_ after school.
Tuesday	Go to the _2_. Find books about Arthur.
Wednesday	Choose a favorite Arthur _3_.
Thursday	Write a book report.
Friday	The report is _4_ today!

COMPOUND WORDS A *compound word* is a word that is made up of two or more smaller words. *Homework* is a compound word.

5–10. Go on a compound-word search. List compound words that name objects in your classroom. Compare your list with a partner's list.

Name _____

WHAT'S IN A WORD?

Scientists use descriptive words to name animals. For example, the word *stegosaurus* comes from the Greek words *stegos*, which means "roof," and *sauros*, which means "lizard." Put the words together and you describe a dinosaur with plates of bone like roof tiles down its back.

1–3. Write the dinosaur names for the pictures. The hints below each picture will help you.

pterodactyl   triceratops   tyrannosaurus

1. *tri-* means "three"
2. *tyrannos* means "tyrant"
3. *pteron* means "wing"

1. _____
2. _____
3. _____

ANIMAL SIMILES Some *similes* describe what a person is like by comparing him or her to what an animal is like. For example, a very smart person could be called *as wise as an owl*. Write the animal name to complete each simile.

| bird |
| mouse |
| fox |

4. as sly as a _____
5. as free as a _____
6. as quiet as a _____

4. _____
5. _____
6. _____

WITH A PARTNER Draw a tic-tac-toe grid. Write a Spelling Word in each square. As you play the game, say the Spelling Word before you mark *X* or *O*. Make new grids, using Spelling Words from other lessons.

tell	went	~~left~~
head	next	hand
bread	nap	act

Integrated Spelling

LESSON 1   13

SPELLING WORDS

1. job
2. spot
3. ring
4. hunt
5. still
6. drop
7. shut
8. such
9. drink
10. truck
11. clock
12. think

Look for other words with the short *i*, short *o*, and short *u* sounds. You might find *win* in a sports article. Perhaps you will find *rock* or *bulb* in a science book.

13. _____
14. _____
15. _____

Words with Short *i*, Short *o*, and Short *u*

Each Spelling Word has the short *i*, the short *o*, or the short *u* sound. Look at the letters that spell those sounds.

Sort the Spelling Words in a way that will help you remember them. Three example words are given.

short i — big
ring
still
drink
think
clock

short o — top
job
spot
drop

short u — bus
truck
hunt
such
shut

▶ The short *i* sound can be spelled *i*.
▶ The short *o* sound can be spelled *o*.
▶ The short *u* sound can be spelled *u*.

14 LESSON 2   Integrated Spelling

Name _____

Strategy Workshop

SPELLING CLUES: Comparing Spellings

When you're not sure how to spell a word, try writing it in different ways. Choose the way that looks correct.

Look at each of the two possible spellings. Write the way that looks correct.

1. dringk   drink
2. spot   sput
3. hunt   hunte
4. rin   ring
5. clok   clock
6. sutch   such

7–11. Choose each word that looks right to complete this comic strip.

I like my new (7. job/jub) working in a marshmallow factory!

I guess there will be a (8. drawp/drop) in the number of boxes of marshmallows today!

Ugh. I don't feel well. I'll (9. schut/shut) off the machine now.

It was only a dream. But I (10. stil/still) don't feel well.

Whoops! I (11. think/thingk) I ate my pillow!

FUN WITH WORDS Do the word math to write a Spelling Word.

12. tr + puck – p = _____

1. drink
2. spot
3. hunt
4. ring
5. clock
6. SUCH
7. JOB
8. drop
9. shut
10. still
11. think
12. TRUCK

Integrated Spelling   LESSON 2   15

Sleep
WORDS

brains
healthy
physical
re-energizes

SPELLING LOG Think about how you might use these words in your writing, and add them to your Spelling Log.

1. _____
2. _____
3. _____
4. _____

5. _____
6. _____
7. _____
8. _____

9. _____
10. _____

Name _____

Vocabulary WordShop

Write a Sleep Word for each description below.

1. This word means "gives energy again."
2. These control the actions of our bodies.
3. This word means "having to do with the body" and comes from the Latin word *physica*.
4. If you are this word, your body is free from illness.

5–8. What other words about sleeping and dreaming do you know? Write them on the lines at the left.

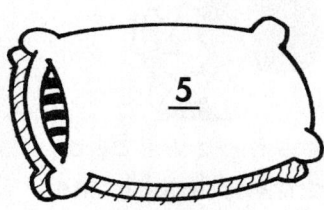 
 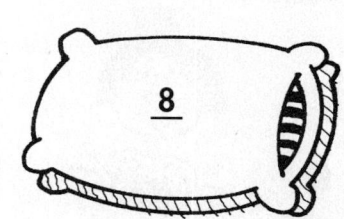

WHAT'S IN A WORD?

The word *ring* has many meanings. You might say that a story does not *ring* true. When something doesn't *ring* true, it doesn't sound or seem true. The word *ring* can also mean a telephone call. Instead of telling your friend, "I'll give you a call," you could say, "I'll give you a *ring*."

9–10. How many other meanings can you think of for the word *ring*? Work with a partner to list two.

Name _____

SOUND WORDS Some words come from sounds. The word *ring* makes the same sound as a bell ringing. Choose a word from the box to match each picture clue.

| boom | buzz | flutter | gurgle | sizzle | zip |

1. _____
2. _____
3. _____
4. _____
5. _____
6. _____

DICTIONARY Write each group of words in alphabetical order. If the first letters of the words are the same, look at the second letters.

7. fly
   swoop
   mouse
   breakfast

8. free
   falcon
   flee
   forest

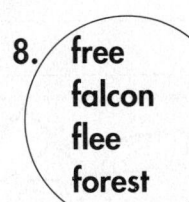

7. _____
   _____
   _____
   _____

8. _____
   _____
   _____
   _____

WRITE TONGUE TWISTERS Use the Spelling Words to write tongue twisters. Here is an example: *Sam shut Sue's shutters in the sunshine.* See whether your classmates can say the tongue twisters fast.

Integrated Spelling

SPELLING WORDS

1. tie
2. soap
3. know
4. lie
5. grow
6. rise
7. stone
8. sight
9. tight
10. goal
11. white
12. close

Look for other words with the long *i* and long *o* sounds. You might find *line* in your math book. You might find *slice* or *toast* in a recipe.

13. _____
14. _____
15. _____

Words with Long *i* and Long *o*

Each Spelling Word has the long *i* or the long *o* sound. Look at the letters that spell those sounds.

Sort the Spelling Words in a way that will help you remember them. Two example words are given.

▶ The long *i* sound can be spelled *ie*, *i–e*, or *igh*.
▶ The long *o* sound can be spelled *oa*, *o–e*, or *ow*.

Name _____

Strategy Workshop

SPELLING CLUES: Rhyming Words Think about the sound of the word. Does it rhyme with another word you know? Is the spelling pattern familiar?

Circle the word or words that rhyme with the underlined word in each row. Write the rhyming words.

1.	<u>chose</u>	close	choose	coin
2–3.	<u>pie</u>	pick	tie	lie
4–5.	<u>fight</u>	sight	tight	slip
6–7.	<u>blow</u>	know	blouse	grow

8-11. Complete this tale based on a story by Aesop. Use the rhyming words in parentheses to help you complete the story with Spelling Words.

The crow had the (foal) __8__ of getting water. He dropped a (bone) __9__ into the (bite) __10__ pitcher. He dropped another and another until he saw the water (wise) __11__ to the top. Then he took a drink.

1. _____
2. _____
3. _____
4. _____
5. _____
6. _____
7. _____

8. _____
9. _____
10. _____
11. _____

FUN WITH WORDS
Write a Spelling Word to complete the caption and make a rhyme.

12. Pass the _____, antelope!

12. _____

Integrated Spelling

Community
WORDS

elders
village
townsfolk
mayor

SPELLING LOG Think about how you might use these words in your writing, and add them to your Spelling Log.

1. _____
2. _____
3. _____
4. _____

5. _____
6. _____

7. _____
8. _____

9. _____

Vocabulary WordShop

Write a Community Word that means the same as the words in parentheses in the town notice.

Town Notice
The __1__ (head of town government) has arranged a special celebration to honor the __2__ (older persons) of this __3__ (small town). All __4__ (people living in the town) are invited to attend.

EXACT NOUNS A noun names a person, place, or thing. An exact noun gives more information. *People* and *person* are nouns. *Mayor, elders,* and *townsfolk* are more exact nouns.

Write an exact noun from the box to name each person pictured below.

grandfather   painter   doctor   captain   sisters

5.
6.
7.
8.
9.

Name _____

DICTIONARY An entry word in a dictionary is a word in dark print followed by its meaning. Entry words are in alphabetical order.

> **town** [toun] *n.* an area with many houses and other buildings, in which people live and work: **He lives in Rye, which is a small *town* outside New York City.**

Look up each word in the Spelling Dictionary. Write the entry word that comes after it.

1. down
2. soil
3. wore
4. before

WHAT'S IN A WORD?

Has anyone ever told you that you're *a sight for sore eyes*? It didn't mean that the person's eyes hurt. It's an expression that means that seeing someone is cause for relief or joy.

5. Describe a situation in which you might say to someone, "You're a sight for sore eyes!"

WITH A PARTNER On a separate sheet of paper, write six Spelling Words to make a word-search puzzle like the one below. Write the words across or down. Fill in the empty spaces with letters. The letters you add should not spell words. Trade puzzles with a classmate, and solve each other's puzzle.

1. _____
2. _____
3. _____
4. _____

5. _____
_____
_____
_____
_____
_____
_____

f	d	k	t	i	l	o
e	w	h	i	t	e	b
q	l	n	g	r	o	w
s	i	g	h	t	c	h
d	e	o	t	i	e	m

Integrated Spelling　　　　　　LESSON 3　21

SPELLING WORDS

1. face
2. meet
3. way
4. deep
5. real
6. green
7. gray
8. paint
9. same
10. these
11. clean
12. raise

Look for other words with long *a* and long *e* sounds to add to the lists. You might find *hail* or *sleet* in a science article. Perhaps you would find *trail* or *east* in a social studies book.

13. _____
14. _____
15. _____

Words with Long *a* and Long *e*

Each Spelling Word has the long *a* or the long *e* sound. Look at the letters that spell those sounds.

Sort the Spelling Words in a way that will help you remember them. Two example words are given.

long e
green

long a
rain

▶ The long *a* sound can be spelled *a–e*, *ay*, or *ai*.
▶ The long *e* sound can be spelled *ee*, *ea*, or *e–e*.

Name _____

Strategy Workshop

PROOFREADING: Working Together When you proofread, work with a partner. Read the words aloud as your partner looks at the spelling. Then switch jobs.

Work with a partner to circle the six Spelling Words that do not look right to you. Write the correct spelling for each one.

1. fase   meet
2. way   depe
3. real   grein
4. grai   paint
5. same   cleen
6. these   rayze

7–11. With a partner, proofread this interview. Circle the five words that have spelling errors. Write the correct spelling for each word.

It's a rele pleasure to meit you. Can you tell us the waiy that you come up with ideas for your pictures?

When I play with my paignt tools—brushes and colors—many ideas pop into my head. Theese ideas often show up in my work.

FUN WITH WORDS Write a Spelling Word to complete this riddle.

Why does Rachel look to one side and then the other when entering a room?
Because she can't look both ways at the __12__ time!

1. _____
2. _____
3. _____
4. _____
5. _____
6. _____

7. _____
8. _____
9. _____
10. _____
11. _____

12. _____

Integrated Spelling   LESSON 4   23

Name _____

Vocabulary WordShop

Art WORDS

artwork
sketched
studio
supplies

SPELLING LOG Think about how you might use these words in your writing, and add them to your Spelling Log.

1. _____
2. _____
3. _____
4. _____

Use the Art Words to complete or write headings for the groups of words in the web.

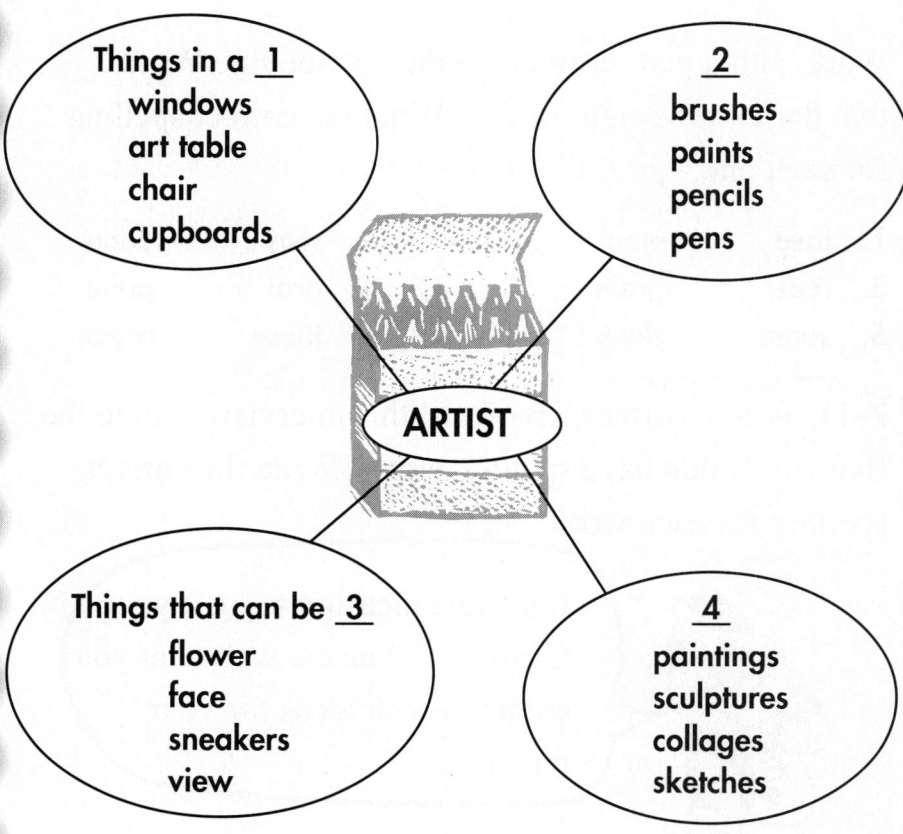

Things in a __1__
windows
art table
chair
cupboards

__2__
brushes
paints
pencils
pens

Things that can be __3__
flower
face
sneakers
view

__4__
paintings
sculptures
collages
sketches

ARTIST

Write a new heading for the web, and list other art words that fit under your heading.

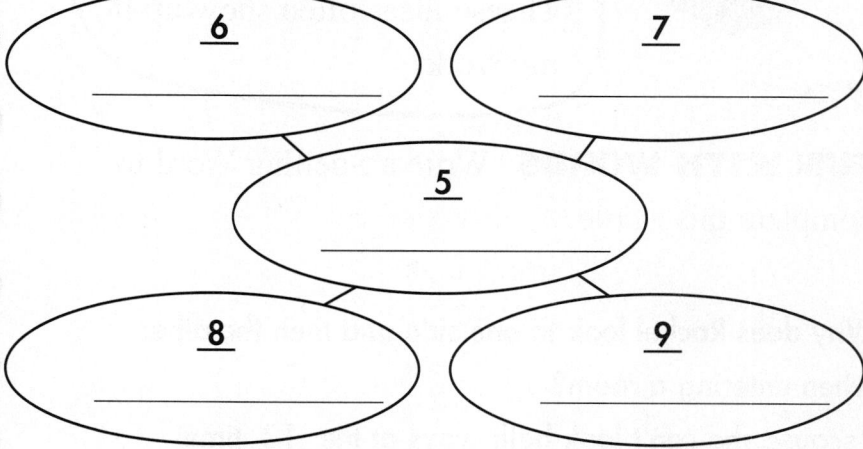

5. _____
6. _____
7. _____
8. _____
9. _____

Name _____

WHAT'S IN A WORD?

When Jerry Pinkney was young, he sketched anything that stood still. The word *sketch* comes from the Dutch word *schets* and means "quick, rough drawing." When you *sketch*, you work quickly and do not pay attention to details.

1. Have you ever heard someone say that a plan or an article is *sketchy*? What do you think the person meant? Write your ideas on the lines.

DICTIONARY Entry words in a dictionary are written as base words. If you want to know the meaning of the word *sketched,* look up the base word, *sketch.* If you want to know the meaning of the word *supplies,* look up the base word, *supply.*

If you wanted to look up the words in dark print below, what words would you look up in the dictionary? Write the base word from the box for each of the words below.

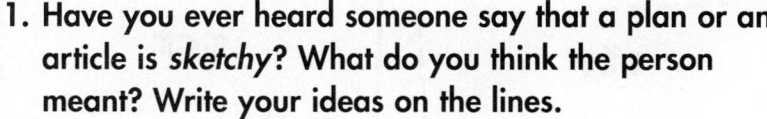

| paint | win | dive | climb |

2. **diving**   3. **winning**
4. **painted** 5. **climbed**

TRY IT OUT Add the letters that spell the vowel sounds to write Spelling Words.

6. g r _ _ n   7. s _ m _
8. r _ _ s _   9. m _ _ t
10. c l _ _ n   11. g r _ _
12. t h _ s _   13. w _ _
14. r _ _ l

1. _____
   _____
   _____
   _____
   _____

2. _____
3. _____
4. _____
5. _____
6. _____
7. _____
8. _____
9. _____
10. _____
11. _____
12. _____
13. _____
14. _____

Integrated Spelling   **LESSON 4   25**

SPELLING WORDS

1. street
2. strike
3. spray
4. screen
5. spread
6. burst
7. scream
8. strong
9. sprout
10. string
11. scratch
12. strange

Look for other words with the consonant cluster *str, scr, spr,* or final *st* to add to the lists. You might find *spring* or *first* in an article about bicycles, and *stream* or *straight* in a map lesson.

13. _____
14. _____
15. _____

Consonant Clusters

Each Spelling Word has the sounds *str, scr, spr,* or final *st*. Look at the letters that spell those sounds.

Sort the Spelling Words in a way that will help you remember them.

▶ Many words have consonant clusters. *Str, scr, spr,* and final *st* are some common ones. Learn the letters that spell these sounds.

Name _____

Strategy Workshop

SPELLING CLUES: Guessing and Checking

When you are not sure how to spell a word, make a guess. After you try out your own spelling, check to see whether you are right.

Look at the two possible spellings. Circle the six words that are misspelled. Then check and write the correct spelling for each word.

1. srtike   strike
2. sprout   srpout
3. skrach   scratch
4. strong   tsrong
5. sreen   screen
6. strange   srange

1. _____
2. _____
3. _____
4. _____
5. _____
6. _____

7–11. Complete this draft of the story below. Circle the five misspelled words in the story. Then write the words correctly. If you are not sure how to spell a word, guess and check.

Our Banner

The children on our (7. street/srteet) decided to create something beautiful. We (8. srpead/spread) a sheet over a wall. Mr. James showed us how to make paint (9. rspay/spray) from a can. You should have heard the little children (10. scream/skreem) when a (11. burst/burts) of color came out! I couldn't wait for my turn.

7. _____
8. _____
9. _____
10. _____
11. _____

FUN WITH WORDS

Use a Spelling Word to complete this riddle.

12. Why did the dinosaur bring _____ to the baseball game? He wanted to tie up the score!

12. _____

Integrated Spelling   LESSON 5   27

Creativity
WORDS

imagine
fantasy
vivid
hue

SPELLING LOG Think about how you would use these words in your writing, and add them to your Spelling Log.

1. _____
2. _____
3. _____
4. _____

5. _____
6. _____
7. _____
8. _____

Name _____

Vocabulary WordShop

Follow the path through this theme park. Use the Creativity Words to complete the conversations along the way. The words in parentheses will help you.

Welcome to Adventure Park, where your wildest __1__ (playful imagination) dreams can come true.

This is Dinosaur Land. Inside you will __2__ (picture or pretend) that you have gone back in time.

Come ride to Paradise Mountain, where the flowers are __3__ (bright) lollipops and the waterfalls are fruit punch.

Have you ever wanted to ride a golden horse or a copper camel? In Animal Kingdom, we have animals of every __4__ (shade of color) imaginable.

5–8. Design your own attraction for Adventure Park. Write the name of your attraction, and tell what guests could do inside.

Name _____

ACTION WORDS What do a *wrapper* and a *worm* have in common? Complete these instructions to find out. For each blank, write the best action word from the box.

```
place    push    sprinkle    wiggle    remove    watch
```

First, __1__ the paper that covers a straw to one end.
Then, __2__ the crumpled wrapper, and __3__ it on the table.
Next, __4__ a drop or two of water on the wrapper.
Last, __5__ the paper wrapper __6__ just like a worm!

WHAT'S IN A WORD?

The word *scientific* comes from the Latin words *scientia*, which means "knowledge," and *facere*, which means "to make." Put them together, and you have "making knowledge."

7. Write about something scientific you have done. Tell what you learned from it.

8. With a classmate, make a list of scientific words. Write them on the lines.

TRY THIS! Choose five Spelling Words that are hard for you to remember. Write each word on a separate sheet of paper, leaving space between the letters of the word. Then cut the words apart so that each letter is on a separate square of paper. Mix up the letters. Then put them together to form the Spelling Words. When you have finished, check to make sure you have spelled each word correctly.

1. _____
2. _____
3. _____
4. _____
5. _____
6. _____

7. _____
_____
_____
_____
_____
_____

8. _____
_____
_____
_____
_____
_____
_____

Integrated Spelling

Name _____

Practice Test

A. Read each sentence. Find the correctly spelled word that completes each sentence. On the answer sheet, mark the letter that is next to that word.

Example: Did you _____ the truth?
    A teel   B teall   C tell

1. I want to _____ in a play.
    A akt   B act   C ect

2. This is my _____ drawing.
    A best   B bast   C beest

3. My crayons are _____ to my markers.
    A naxt   B next   C neaxt

4. Do you _____ this story is good?
    A think   B thonk   C thenk

5. Which _____ do you want?
    A jub   B jeob   C job

6. I have to _____ for my tap shoes.
    A hun   B hunt   C hont

7. We were sitting in a _____.
    A rong   B ring   C reeng

8. What makes those snowflakes _____?
    A white   B wite   C whight

9. I _____ it will be hard.
    A knoaw   B knoge   C know

10. I will _____ down over here.
    A ligh   B liye   C lie

EXAMPLE
A B **C**

ANSWERS
1. A B C
2. A B C
3. A B C
4. A B C
5. A B C
6. A B C
7. A B C
8. A B C
9. A B C
10. A B C

Name _____

B. Read each sentence. Find the correctly spelled word to complete each sentence. On the answer sheet, mark the letter that is next to that word.

1. What is your _____?
   A gowl   B goal   C gole

2. That's a beautiful _____.
   A stone   B stown   C stoan

3. We need to _____ some money.
   A rayse   B raise   C rase

4. We like the _____ music.
   A saim   B saym   C same

5. Which _____ shall we go?
   A whae   B way   C wai

6. I have to _____ my brushes.
   A clean   B cleen   C clene

7. How _____ is that water?
   A deap   B deep   C depe

8. Does my mask look _____?
   A srange   B srtange   C strange

9. Shine the light on the _____.
   A screen   B screan   C screne

10. She _____ into the room.
    A berst   B burts   C burst

ANSWERS

1. A B C
2. A B C
3. A B C
4. A B C
5. A B C
6. A B C
7. A B C
8. A B C
9. A B C
10. A B C

Integrated Spelling   LESSON 6 • REVIEW   31

Unit 1: Writing Activities

WORDS TO WATCH FOR

anything
beautiful
goes
send
gets
inside
lunch
Miss

What's New with You?

Who do you think is creative? A storyteller, a weaver, and a school chef who makes your favorite lunch are all creative in different ways. Write a friendly letter to a person you think is creative. Tell the person what you like about his or her work. You could also ask questions to learn more about the person and his or her talents. Include all five parts of a letter. When you have finished your letter, address an envelope for it.

Tips for Spelling Success

- Before you send your letter, ask a classmate to help you proofread it. Together, look for words that might be misspelled.
- Some Words to Watch For are on the left.

Tips for Spelling Success

- Help your classmates read your chart by using correct spelling.
- If you are not sure how to spell a word, write it a few ways on another sheet of paper.
- Choose the way that looks correct.

Did You Know?

The books you have been reading are filled with interesting information about creativity. Make a "Did You Know?" chart. On the left side of the chart, write questions such as "Did you know that everyone dreams?" On the right side, write the name of the book in which you found the information. As you read other books, add more questions. Invite classmates to add to your chart, too!

Name _____

Creative You

Have you ever painted a picture or written a tune? Did you ever solve a problem in an interesting way or come up with a creative plan? Write a paragraph about a time when you created something you were proud of. Use details to help the reader picture the event and your special creation. After you have revised your paragraph, copy it. Bind it with those of your classmates to make a class book called "Creativity at Work."

Tips for Spelling Success
- It is difficult to read something when the words are misspelled.
- One way to make sure your words are spelled correctly is by proofreading your first draft.
- When you proofread, circle words that do not look right.
- Then check the spelling.

Rhyme Time!

Can you solve these word puzzles? On each line, write a word that rhymes with *tone*.

This is another word for a rock. _____
Call me on the _____.
Give the dog a _____.
It holds ice cream. _____
This means "all by yourself." _____

Tips for Spelling Success
- To check your answers, see whether they follow the same spelling pattern as the rhyming word *tone*.

Integrated Spelling   LESSON 6 • REVIEW   33

SPELLING WORDS

1. knew
2. write
3. knees
4. phone
5. knife
6. wrote
7. laugh
8. wrong
9. known
10. knock
11. rough
12. telephone

Look for other words with *kn, wr, gh,* or *ph* to add to the lists. You might find *knight* or *knock* in a fairy tale, *wrestle* and *wrist* in a sports article, or *photograph* in the front of a magazine or a nonfiction book.

13. _____
14. _____
15. _____

Words with *kn, wr, gh,* and *ph*

Each Spelling Word has a consonant pair that spells a single sound. Look at the letter pairs that spell the *n*, the *r*, and the *f* sounds.

Sort the Spelling Words in a way that will help you remember them.

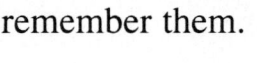

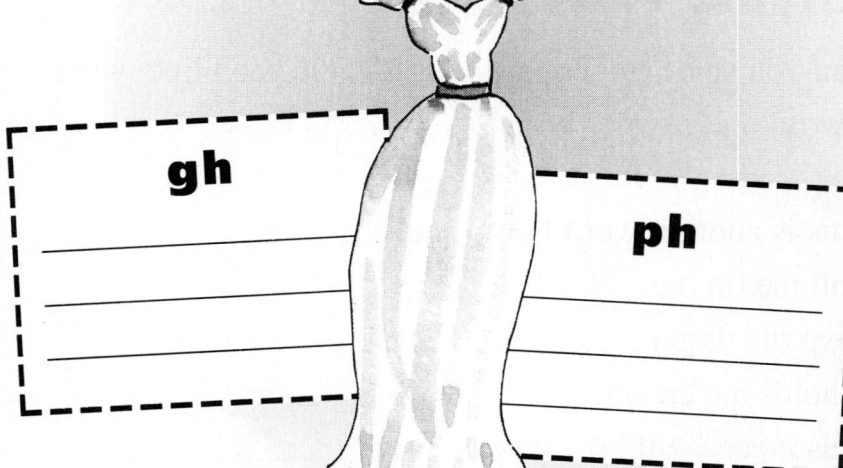

▶ The consonant sound *n* can be spelled *kn*.
▶ The consonant sound *r* can be spelled *wr*.
▶ The consonant sound *f* can be spelled *gh* or *ph*.

34 LESSON 7

Integrated Spelling

Name _____

Strategy Workshop

SPELLING CLUES: Word Shapes Pay attention to the shapes of words. To remember the spelling of a word, draw its shape.

Think of a Spelling Word to fit each word shape. Use the clues to help you. Then write the words on the numbered lines.

1. Get down on your hands and ____.
2. You need a fork, a ____, and a spoon.
3. This stone is as ____ as sandpaper.
4. Call her on the ____.
5. I ____ it!

1. _____
2. _____
3. _____
4. _____
5. _____

Complete the rules. Write the Spelling Word that fits in each word shape.

Rules for Visiting a Duchess

6. Always call on the ____ first.
7. Do not arrive at the ____ time.
8. You must ____ loudly on the castle door.
9. Always ____ at her jokes.
10. Don't forget to ____ a thank-you note afterward.

6. _____
7. _____
8. _____
9. _____
10. _____

FUN WITH WORDS Write two Spelling Words to complete the cartoon.

How could I have __11__ you were coming?

I __12__ you a letter. See, I have it right here!

11. _____
12. _____

Integrated Spelling

Royalty
* WORDS *

ball
duchess
palace
aristocrats

SPELLING LOG Think about how you might use these words in your writing, and add them to your Spelling Log.

1. _____
2. _____
3. _____
4. _____

5. _____
6. _____
7. _____
8. _____

Name _____

Vocabulary WordShop

Here is an imaginary thank-you note that Irene might have sent the duchess. Complete the note by using each picture clue to write a Royalty Word.

Dear 1 Du +  ,

Thank you for inviting me to the 2

 3 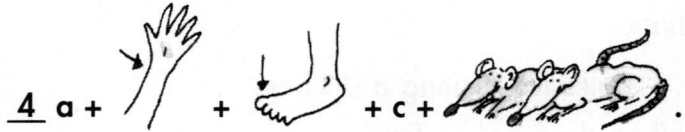 . I enjoyed meeting the

 4 a + ✋ + 🦶 + c + 🐭🐭 .

Fondly,
Irene

5–8. Write four other royalty words you know.

WHAT'S IN A WORD?

Aristocrats are people with high rank who usually have more money and privileges than other people in a society. The word *aristocrats* comes from the Greek words *aristos*, meaning "the best," and *kratos*, meaning "power." Put the two together, and you have "the best people to have power."

Name _____

WORD HISTORIES All groups of people have leaders of one kind or another. Can you match the words in the box to their word histories?

> emperor   chief   president   queen

1. This word comes from the Latin word *praesidere* and means "to sit in front of."
2. This word comes from the Latin word *imperare* and means "to command."
3. This word comes from the Old English word *cwen* and means "female ruler."
4. This word comes from the Latin word *caput* and means "leader" or "boss."

1. _____
2. _____
3. _____
4. _____

SYNONYMS *Synonyms* are words with the same meaning or nearly the same meaning. The words *laugh* and *chuckle* are examples of synonyms. Choose a synonym from the box to replace each word below in parentheses.

> brave   story   gown   friends   ball   trudging

Dear Irene,
    You are so (5. courageous)! I can't imagine (6. walking) through a snowstorm with the (7. dress). I will tell all my (8. pals) the (9. tale) of how you came to my (10. dance).
                    Yours truly,
                    The Duchess

11. What other synonyms can you think of for the word *laugh*? Write several on the lines.

5. _____
6. _____
7. _____
8. _____
9. _____
10. _____
11. _____
    _____
    _____
    _____

PLAY "TWENTY QUESTIONS" Write a Spelling Word on a piece of paper. Have a partner ask up to ten yes-or-no questions to determine which word you wrote. Score one point for each question your partner asks. Take turns writing Spelling Words and asking questions. The person with the lower score wins.

Integrated Spelling   LESSON 7   37

SPELLING WORDS

1. chin
2. push
3. sharp
4. much
5. peach
6. shook
7. child
8. where
9. wash
10. wheat
11. choose
12. chance

Look for other words with *sh*, *ch*, or *wh* to add to the lists. You might see *shark*, *whale*, or *fish* in a book about the sea. You are likely to find *which*, *chart*, and *shape* in your math book.

13. _____
14. _____
15. _____

Words with *sh*, *ch*, and *wh*

Each Spelling Word has the sound *sh*, *ch*, or *hw*. Look at the letters that spell those sounds.

Sort the Spelling Words in a way that will help you remember them.

▶ The *sh* sound can be spelled *sh*.
▶ The *ch* sound can be spelled *ch*.
▶ The *hw* sound can be spelled *wh*.

Name _____

Strategy Workshop

SPELLING RULES: Sounds and Letters Say the word to yourself. Close your eyes and picture the way it is spelled. Does it have more letters than sounds? Which letter pair spells a single sound?

Add the letters *ch*, *sh*, or *wh*, and then write the Spelling Word.

1. _ _ a n c e   2. _ _ e a t   3. _ _ o o k
    4. _ _ i n   5. _ _ o o s e

Complete the story. Add the missing letters, and then write the words.

I had begun to (6. wa _ _) the dishes when I heard a sound. It was a (7. _ _ arp) cry—a sound such as a (8. _ _ ild) might make. I decided to see (9. _ _ ere) it was coming from. I was nervous, but I started to (10. pu _ _) the door open. (11. Mu _ _) to my surprise, the sound was coming from a little cat!

FUN WITH WORDS Write a Spelling Word to complete this silly riddle.

What did one worm say to the other?
Meet you at the __12__!

1. _____
2. _____
3. _____
4. _____
5. _____

6. _____
7. _____
8. _____
9. _____
10. _____
11. _____

12. _____

Storm Sound
WORDS

hollered
whined
whooped
cracked

SPELLING LOG Think about how you might use these words in your writing, and add them to your Spelling Log.

1. _____
2. _____
3. _____
4. _____

5. _____

Vocabulary WordShop

Write a Storm Sound Word that tells what sound each picture represents. Use the clues to help you.

1. cried in a high, complaining voice
2. comes from the Latin word *hola*, which means "stop there!"
3. rhymes with *backed*
4. a sound of excitement

WHAT'S IN A WORD?

Thomas had to *keep his chin up* during the storm. Keeping your chin up means "keeping your spirits up even when things are not going well." When you've had a disappointment, tell yourself "Chin up!"

5. Complete this sentence: *You should keep your chin up when* ____ .

Name _____

IDIOMS An *idiom* is an expression that does not mean exactly what it says. *Stay on your toes* is one example. Write a word to complete each idiom.

| nose | eye | foot | hand |

1. We don't see ____ to eye.
2. It was right under my ____.
3. "Give this group a big ____."
4. I'm putting my ____ down.

1. _____
2. _____
3. _____
4. _____

DICTIONARY At the top of each dictionary page are two *guide words*. They tell the first and last entry words that are listed on the page.

Write the Spelling Words you would find on a dictionary page that has each pair of guide words shown here.

5–6. rose   shop
7–9. valley   worry

MAKE A WORD CHAIN Start by writing one Spelling Word, across or down. Then, using a letter in the first word, write another Spelling Word, across or down.

5. _____
6. _____
7. _____
8. _____
9. _____

Integrated Spelling   LESSON 8   41

SPELLING WORDS

1. cool
2. foot
3. zoo
4. good
5. moon
6. cook
7. noon
8. soup
9. shoe
10. wood
11. loose
12. scoop

Look for other words with the vowel sounds you hear in *zoo* and *good* to add to the lists. You might find *route* on a map. *Hoot* and *loon* might be found in a science article about birds.

13. _____
14. _____
15. _____

Words Like *zoo* and *good*

Each Spelling Word has the vowel sound that you hear in *zoo* or *good*. Look at the letters that spell those sounds.

Sort the Spelling Words in a way that will help you remember them. Two example words are given.

▶ The vowel sound that you hear in *zoo* can be spelled *oo*, *ou*, or *oe*.

▶ The vowel sound that you hear in *good* can be spelled *oo*.

Name _____

Strategy Workshop

PROOFREADING: Using a Dictionary When you proofread, circle words you are unsure of. Use a dictionary to check the spellings. The guide words can help you locate a word more quickly.

Which Spelling Words do not look right to you? Circle the words with spelling errors, and look them up in a dictionary. Use guide words to help you find the words. Then write the correct spellings.

1. noon   soop   2. cool   shoo
3. luse   scoop   4. zou   good
5. moon   couk   6. woode   foot

7–11. Complete this diary entry. Write the Spelling Word you would find on a dictionary page that has the guide words in parentheses and completes the entry.

June 3
   I wanted to be brave, so I started on a hike by myself at (7. nation, north). The air was (8. clock, dance), and the sun on my back felt great. Everything would have been perfect if I hadn't caught my (9. face, force) on that tree root. I thought I was flying to the (10. match, morning)! It's a (11. form, happy) thing I wasn't hurt. Next time, I'll be brave with a buddy.

FUN WITH WORDS Choose a Spelling Word to complete the riddle.

   How do you make an elephant float?

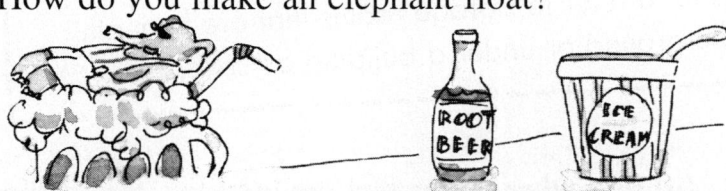

12. Just _____ up some ice cream. Put it in a glass with some milk and some root beer. Then add one elephant.

1. _____
2. _____
3. _____
4. _____
5. _____
6. _____

7. _____
8. _____
9. _____
10. _____
11. _____

12. _____

Integrated Spelling   LESSON 9   43

Worry
WORDS

shake
sweat
rumbling
trembling

SPELLING LOG Think about how you might use these words in your writing, and add them to your Spelling Log.

1. _____
2. _____
3. _____
4. _____

5. _____
6. _____
7. _____
8. _____

Vocabulary WordShop

Use the Worry Words to complete the story about this picture.

Usually, I <u> 1 </u> when that bully talks to me. But yesterday, even though my knees were <u> 2 </u> and my stomach was <u> 3 </u>, I just stood there and stared her in the eye. This time, she started to wipe away her <u> 4 </u>!

WHAT'S IN A WORD?

In the story the boys find a kitten in the *cellar* of a building. The word *cellar* comes from the Latin word *cella*, which means "storeroom." We tend to refer to storage rooms that are beneath the ground or under a building as *cellars*.

5–8. List four other places that are used for storing things.

Name _____

CLIPPED WORDS Over the years, some words have been shortened, or clipped. *Zoo* is a clipped word for *zoological gardens*.

Read what the boy in "Lester's Dog" may have written to Mr. Frank. Circle the five words that we usually use in their clipped forms today. Let the words in the box help you.

| phone | fridge | vet | taxi | exam |

> May 19
>
> Dear Mr. Frank,
>   I was going to call you on the telephone, but I decided to write instead. I hope you like the kitten. I didn't take it to the veterinarian, so you may want to put it in a taxicab and take it for an examination. That kitty was really hungry! Does it come running every time you open the refrigerator?
>   Well, that's all for now!
>   Kira

1–5. Write the clipped words in the order in which their longer forms appear in the letter.

6. What other clipped words do you know? Write them on the lines.

TRY IT OUT Write a Spelling Word for each clue.

7. This word has four letters, has the letter *u*, and rhymes with *group*.
8. This word has five letters, has the letter *e*, and rhymes with *moose*.
9. This word has four letters, has the letter *k*, and rhymes with *book*.
10. This word has four letters, has the letter *e*, and rhymes with *do*.

1. _____
2. _____
3. _____
4. _____
5. _____

6. _____
   _____
   _____
   _____
   _____

7. _____
8. _____
9. _____
10. _____

Integrated Spelling   LESSON 9   45

Words Like *small*

SPELLING WORDS

1. also
2. draw
3. walk
4. long
5. cause
6. lost
7. paws
8. small
9. always
10. soft
11. almost
12. talk

Look for other words like *small* to add to the lists. You might find *song* in a music book. You might find *all* and *cost* in your math book.

13. _____
14. _____
15. _____

Name _____

Each Spelling Word has the vowel sound you hear in *small*. Look at the letters that spell that sound.

Sort the Spelling Words in a way that will help you remember them. Five example words are given.

ball or chalk

dog

saw

pause

▶ The vowel sound you hear in *small* can be spelled *a*, *al*, *o*, *aw*, or *au*.

46 LESSON 10

Integrated Spelling

Name _____

Strategy Workshop

SPELLING CLUES: Picture Words If you want to remember how a word is spelled, write the word as a picture. Here are some examples:

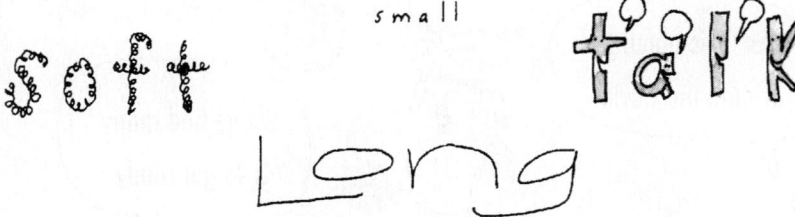

Look at the pictures above. Then look at the two possible spellings of each word. Write the correct spelling.

1. sauft   soft   2. long   lawng
3. small   smal   4. tauk   talk

5–11. Circle the seven misspelled Spelling Words in this wish. Then write the correct spelling of each word. If you can, write some of these Spelling Words as picture words, like the ones above.

> I wish I could find my laust puppy with the white paas. I found a puppy that looked awlmost the same as mine. It was the wrong dog. I will tolk to everyone I know and ask if they have seen him. My sister is aulso looking for the puppy. I will awlways think of him. Maybe my wish will come true! Maybe my puppy will drauw closer to home when he gets hungry.

FUN WITH WORDS Follow the directions to write a Spelling Word.

12. c + laugh – l – gh + se =

1. _____
2. _____
3. _____
4. _____

5. _____
6. _____
7. _____
8. _____
9. _____
10. _____
11. _____

12. _____

Integrated Spelling   LESSON 10   47

Name _____

Vocabulary WordShop

Celebration WORDS

pageant
holidays
piñata
rehearsals

SPELLING LOG Think about how you might use these words in your writing, and add them to your Spelling Log.

1. _____
2. _____
3. _____
4. _____

Use the Celebration Words to complete the conversation.

"Our **1** is about **2** around the world."

"We've had many **3** to get ready."

"After our show, we get to break the **4**."

5–8. People celebrate many different winter holidays. Make a list of words from those holidays.

5. _____
6. _____
7. _____
8. _____

WHAT'S IN A WORD?

The word *holiday* comes from an Old English word that meant "holy day." In England long ago, the only days when people didn't work were religious feast days.

9–11. List some of the different foods people eat during the winter holidays.

9. _____
10. _____
11. _____

48 LESSON 10   Integrated Spelling

Name _____

ANTONYMS   An *antonym* is a word that means the opposite of another word.

Soft is an antonym of *loud*.

1–6. Correct this essay about a name. For each underlined word, write an antonym from the star.

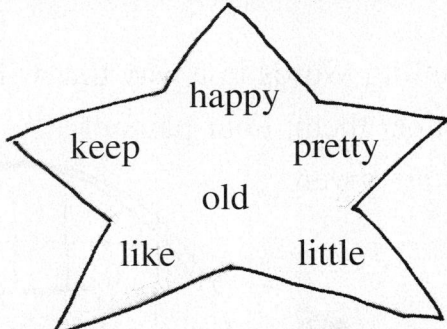

When I was big, I did not hate my name. I thought the name sounded too young. But then I learned that the name Bonita means ugly and that it was my grandmother's name. Now I'm sad with the name. I think I'll discard it!

DICTIONARY   A *definition* tells what an entry word in a dictionary means.

lost [lôst] *adj.* not able to be found

Find these three Spelling Words in your Spelling Dictionary. Write a definition of each.

7. also   8. cause   9. always

WITH A PARTNER   Play a guessing game with the Spelling Words. One partner picks a word and gives a clue, such as "This word begins like *pencil* and belongs to animals." The other partner writes the word *paws*. Take turns giving the clues and guessing the Spelling Words.

1. _____
2. _____
3. _____
4. _____
5. _____
6. _____

7. _____
   _____
   _____
8. _____
   _____
   _____
9. _____
   _____
   _____

Integrated Spelling   LESSON 10   49

SPELLING WORDS

1. smaller
2. finest
3. biggest
4. richer
5. happiest
6. bigger
7. closer
8. nicer
9. nicest
10. longer
11. thinner
12. richest

Look for other words that end with -er and -est to add to the lists. You might find *saddest* in a classmate's story, *rarest* in a social studies article, and *drier* or *driest* in a science article.

13. _____
14. _____
15. _____

Words with -er and -est

Each Spelling Word ends with *-er* or *-est*. Look for changes in the spelling of a word when these endings are added.

Sort the Spelling Words in a way that will help you remember them. Four pairs of example words are given.

▶ If a word ends with two consonants, there are no spelling changes before you add *-er* or *-est*.

▶ If a word ends with *e*, drop the *e* and add *-er* or *-est*.

▶ If a word ends with a single consonant, double the consonant and add *-er* or *-est*.

▶ If a word ends with a consonant and *y*, change the *y* to *i* and add *-er* or *-est*.

Name _____

Strategy Workshop

SPELLING CLUES: Spelling Rules When you want to spell a word that has an ending, think about how the word is spelled without the ending. Then remember the rule for adding an ending to the word.

Add an ending from the box to write a Spelling Word.

-er	-est

1. small   2. fine   3. thin
4. happy   5. long   6. close

7–10. Complete the sentences. Write the correct spellings of the words.

I am (7. riccher/richer) than you.

She is the (8. richest/richiest) one of all.

This horse has a (9. nicer/nicier) jump than my other horse.

This horse has the (10. niciest/nicest) jump of all the horses I've ridden.

FUN WITH WORDS Use two Spelling Words to complete the joke.

The 11 fish gets the worm.

Who's the 12 fish of all?

1. _____
2. _____
3. _____
4. _____
5. _____
6. _____

7. _____
8. _____
9. _____
10. _____

11. _____
12. _____

Integrated Spelling

LESSON 11

Daring
WORDS

brave
positive
courageous
confident

SPELLING LOG Think about how you might use these words in your writing, and add them to your Spelling Log.

1. _____
2. _____
3. _____
4. _____
5. _____
   _____
   _____
   _____
6. _____
   _____
   _____
   _____
   _____
   _____

Vocabulary WordShop

Write the Daring Words in the word shapes to complete each sentence. Then write the words on the lines.

1. Firefighters need to be 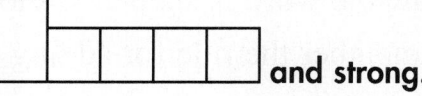 and strong.

2. The President is 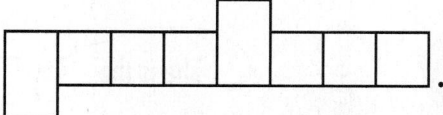 that his bill will pass.

3. The opposite of negative is 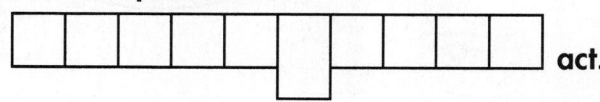.

4. The hero performed a ⬚⬚⬚⬚⬚⬚⬚⬚⬚⬚ act.

5. Write a sentence using some of the Daring Words.

WHAT'S IN A WORD?

You know many story characters who are brave. To be *brave* means "to have courage." Did you also know that words can change meaning over time? In the past the word *brave* has meant "a bully," "a boast or challenge," and "to make splendid."

6. Think about someone you know who did something brave. Write about it on the lines.

52 LESSON 11   Integrated Spelling

Name _____

DICTIONARY The words in a dictionary are in alphabetical order. To find a word in a dictionary, look at the first letter of the word. The Guide Words will help you find this letter's section in the dictionary. Then look at the next letter of the word to help you find the word in the dictionary. Go on to the next letter in the word until you find that word in the dictionary.

br<u>a</u>ve　　　　br<u>e</u>ad　　　　br<u>i</u>ng

Write each group of words in alphabetical order to make a sentence. The first letters of the words are the same, so look at the next letters.

1. courageously　　2. Walden
   cougars　　　　　wires
   Connie　　　　　 wacky
   confident　　　　worries
   cornered　　　　 walks
   　　　　　　　　without

TRY THIS! Unscramble the letters to form Spelling Words.

3. ntenhir　　4. sticen　　5. scorel
6. shapitep　7. sfenit　　8. rallems
9. stigbeg　 10. chreir　 11. inerc

1. _____
   _____
   _____
   _____
   _____

2. _____
   _____
   _____
   _____
   _____
   _____

3. _____
4. _____
5. _____
6. _____
7. _____
8. _____
9. _____
10. _____
11. _____

Integrated Spelling　　　　LESSON 11　53

Name _____

Practice Test

A. Each underlined word in the story below is misspelled. On the answer sheet, mark the letter next to the correct spelling.

    I just <u>nue</u> that my friends would <u>lauph</u> at me when we went to the amusement
       1   2
park. I was <u>awlmost</u> nine years old and still afraid to ride the roller coaster. "What if a
             3
screw on the track comes <u>loese</u>?" I asked my older brother. "What if the mechanic
                            4
doesn't have a <u>shance</u> to make a safety check?"
              5

    "You worry too <u>musch</u>," he said.
               6

    I decided to go on the roller coaster with my friends. We waited in a <u>lawng</u> line to
                                                                       7
ride the <u>bigest</u> roller coaster. I tried to <u>coek</u> up a reason for backing out, but I couldn't.
         8   9
Guess what? I loved riding the roller coaster! It was one of my <u>happyest</u> times!
                                                                            10

ANSWERS

#	A	B	C	D
1.	gnue	knuw	knoo	knew
2.	lauf	laugh	laph	laf
3.	almost	olmast	awmost	aulmost
4.	loce	luse	loose	looze
5.	chanzs	chance	jance	chaince
6.	moch	muhc	much	mutsh
7.	lang	longe	laung	long
8.	biggest	biggist	biggiest	bigyest
9.	kook	cook	couk	coock
10.	happyiest	happest	happiest	hapiest

54   LESSON 12 • REVIEW   Integrated Spelling

Name _____

B. Below are three spellings of each word. On the answer sheet, mark the letter that is next to the correct spelling.

Example: A suft   B sawft   C soft

1. A wronge   B wrong   C rong
2. A phone   B fone   C phoan
3. A shaurp   B charp   C sharp
4. A hweat   B wheet   C wheat
5. A shou   B shoe   C shouw
6. A wood   B woud   C wold
7. A draw   B drauw   C drow
8. A cose   B cawse   C cause
9. A smaler   B smaller C smallier
10. A nicer   B niceer   C nighcer

Integrated Spelling   **LESSON 12 • REVIEW**

Unit 2: Writing Activities

WORDS TO WATCH FOR

cave
reading
aunt
under
belt
climb
using
each other

Tips for Spelling Success

- When writing the names of characters, make sure that you spell each one correctly.
- People's names need to be capitalized.
- Titles such as *Mr.* and *Dr.*, as well as abbreviations, need to begin with a capital letter and have a period at the end of them.

A Courageous Critic

Write a book review about an adventure book you have read. First, tell a little about the book. (Do not spoil any surprises or give away the ending!) Then tell whether you liked the book and why. Express your opinion clearly, and back it up with details from the book. Consult your Spelling Log as you write. Look for persuasive words that will lead your reader to the same conclusion you drew about the book. Book reviews help others find books they will like. Put your review and the reviews of your classmates in a folder. You can look in the folder the next time you want a good book to read.

Tips for Spelling Success

- Make your review easy to read by using correct spelling.
- If you are not sure a word is spelled right, close your eyes and picture the word.
- Does the word have a "silent" letter?
- Some Words to Watch For are on the left.

What's Your Opinion?

Choose one quality you like in a book character. For example, you might like characters who never give up or characters who are brave, clever, or funny. Write the names of five characters you have read about in class who have this quality. Then take a survey to find out which characters your classmates think have the quality you chose. Each time a character is mentioned, put a tally mark next to his or her name. Share your results with the class. You might want to make an award for the character who is mentioned most often.

Tales of Bravery

Think about a time when you were brave. Write a picture book about that time. To help you get started, make a list of five to seven words that describe being brave. Then write your story on scratch paper. Use time-order words to show the order of events. To make your book, use several sheets of paper. Write only a few sentences on each page. Make sure each page includes a sentence you want to illustrate. Then draw pictures on the pages. Bind your picture book and read it to someone who is younger than you.

Tips for Spelling Success

- To create a "picture perfect" book, spell each word correctly.
- When you revise your draft, circle words whose spelling you are not sure of.
- Look up the words in a dictionary. The guide words in the dictionary will help you find the words.

Picture This!

Use the pictures to solve these puzzles. Write the word that solves each puzzle on the line beside it.

s + [hook] = _____

k + [night sky] = _____

[tea bag] + ch = _____

c + [bandage] = _____

Tips for Spelling Success

- Making picture words can help you remember how words are spelled.

SPELLING WORDS

1. joy
2. found
3. soil
4. down
5. out
6. house
7. loud
8. enjoy
9. oil
10. flower
11. point
12. brown

Look for other words with the vowel sounds you hear in *joy* and *down* to add to the lists. You might see *count* and *coin* in your math book, *town* on a map, and *voyage* in a science or social studies article.

13. _____
14. _____
15. _____

Words Like *joy* and *down*

Each Spelling Word has the vowel sound you hear in *joy* or *down*. Look at the letters that spell those sounds.

Sort the Spelling Words in a way that will help you remember them. One example word has been given. Fill in the other one as you are sorting.

boy

▶ The vowel sound you hear in *joy* can be spelled *oy* or *oi*.
▶ The vowel sound you hear in *down* can be spelled *ow* or *ou*.

Name _____

Strategy Workshop

PROOFREADING: Classifying Errors When you proofread, keep a list of your spelling errors. See what kinds of mistakes you usually make, and then work to correct them.

What's wrong with each word in the box? Follow the directions to write the correct spelling.

| dwon   poynt   huose   enjay   laud   oyl |

1–2. Change a vowel to correct two words.
3–4. Change *oy* to *oi* to correct two words.
5–6. Reverse two letters to correct two words.

1. _____
2. _____
3. _____
4. _____
5. _____
6. _____

Proofread these phrases about plants. Circle the five spelling mistakes, and then write the correct spellings.

7. requires healthy soel

8. hardy plant with a brightly colored flawer

9. leaves turn brawn with too much sun

10. can be foond in many different climates

11. easy-to-grow beans—a gardener's jiy

7. _____
8. _____
9. _____
10. _____
11. _____

12. Write the kind of error that was made in all five misspelled words.

12. _____
_____
_____

FUN WITH WORDS Choose a Spelling Word to complete this riddle.

Why didn't Megan talk about the tooth she had pulled by the dentist?

13. It went right __13__ of her head.

13. _____

Integrated Spelling

Real Estate WORDS

- building
- lease
- rent
- office

SPELLING LOG Think about how you might use these words in your writing, and add them to your Spelling Log.

1. _____
2. _____
3. _____
4. _____
5. _____

6. _____
7. _____
8. _____
9. _____
10. _____

Name _____

Vocabulary WordShop

Write a Real Estate Word from the box for each clue.

| building | lease | rent | office |

1. This word names a place where the work of a business is done.

2–3. These words are synonyms and mean "the right to use something for payment."

4. This word names a structure built for people to live in or do things in.

5. Neighbors in City Green rented some land called a lot. What else can be rented? Write your ideas on the lines.

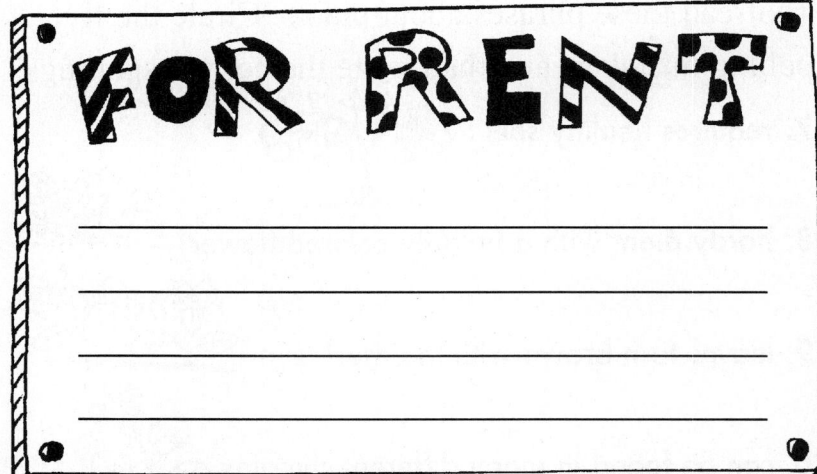

_____
_____
_____
_____

WHAT'S IN A WORD?

In City Green, Old Man Hammer comes *down* the steps, Mr. Rocco lives two houses *down*, and people are cleaning up a lot where a building came *down*. The word *down* comes from the Old English word *afdune*. *Af* meant "from" and *dune* meant "hill." Together they meant "from the hill."

6. What other things can you come down from?

7–10. What things can go down?

Name _____

JOINED WORDS Many words come from combining the word *down* with another word. How many of these words have you heard? Choose words from the box to complete the conversation.

| downpour   downhearted   downplay   downfall |

I wasn't __1__ when I heard this building is being destroyed. It couldn't keep someone dry in a __2__.

Well, all the repairs the building needed were its __3__. But don't __4__ the importance of this building to you. It was your home for a long time.

5–7. What three words can you think of that join *down* with another word?

DICTIONARY The word *point* has more than one meaning. Look up the word in a dictionary. Write the definition that fits each picture.

8.   9.   10.

WITH A PARTNER Play "Memory." Have each player write each Spelling Word on a separate index card. Turn the cards face down. Take turns flipping two cards to try to make matches. If the cards match, keep them. If they don't, turn them face down. The person with more matches at the end of the game wins.

1. _____
2. _____
3. _____
4. _____

5. _____
6. _____
7. _____

8. _____

9. _____

10. _____

Integrated Spelling   LESSON 13   61

Words Like *yard* **and** *air*

Name _____

SPELLING WORDS

1. air
2. bear
3. yard
4. there
5. large
6. wear
7. stare
8. mark
9. share
10. aware
11. hair
12. square

Each Spelling Word has the vowel sound you hear in *yard* or in *air*. Look at the letters that spell those sounds.

Sort the Spelling Words in a way that will help you remember them. One example word has been given. Fill in the other one as you are sorting.

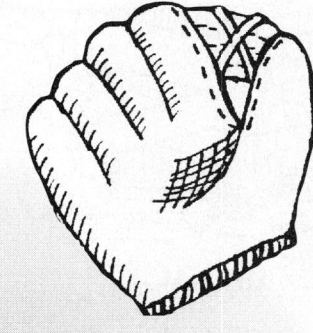

care

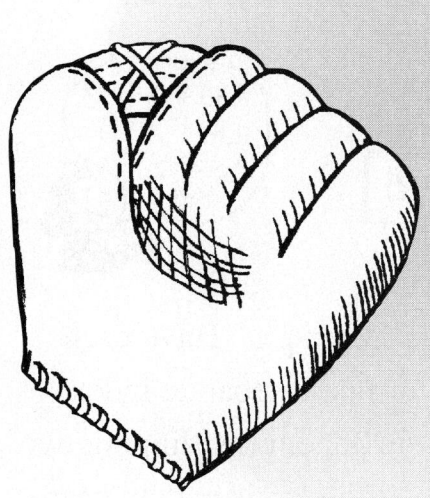

Your Own WORDS

Look for other words like *yard* and *air* to add to the lists. You might find *stars* and *Mars* in a science article. You might find *bar* and *pair* in a math book.

13. _____
14. _____
15. _____

▶ The vowel sound you hear in *yard* can be spelled *ar*.
▶ The vowel sound you hear in *air* can be spelled *air, ere, are,* or *ear*.

62 LESSON 14   Integrated Spelling

Name _____

Strategy Workshop

SPELLING CLUES: Placeholder Spelling

When you want to write a word that you do not know how to spell, write the word the way it sounds and circle it. After you get your ideas down on paper, look up the word in a dictionary.

Look at the six circled words below, spelled the way they sound. Look them up in your Spelling Dictionary. Then write the correct spellings on the lines provided.

1. (skware)   2. (awear)   3. (staire)

4. (marc)   5. (bair)   6. (haer)

7–11. Write a Spelling Word to fill in each blank and complete the baseball poster. Then look up each word in the Spelling Dictionary to see whether you have spelled it correctly.

Join the Jets!
Come join our team and __7__ in the glory of winning. Tryouts will be in the school __8__. You'll want to have plenty to drink, so bring a __9__ water bottle. We hope to see you __10__! Please __11__ comfortable clothing.

FUN WITH WORDS Complete this riddle with a Spelling Word.

What do frogs and baseball players have in common? They both catch flies in the __12__!

1. _____
2. _____
3. _____
4. _____
5. _____
6. _____

7. _____
8. _____
9. _____
10. _____
11. _____

12. _____

Integrated Spelling

Name _____

Baseball WORDS

centerfield
singled
grounded
inning

SPELLING LOG Think about how you might use these words in your writing, and add them to your Spelling Log.

1. _____
2. _____
3. _____
4. _____

Vocabulary WordShop

Write the Baseball Words to complete the sports article below. Use the words in parentheses as clues.

THAT'S TEAMWORK!

In the ninth (**1. one part of a baseball game**), Miguel Fernandez (**2. hit a baseball so that it rolled or bounced**) a ball to third. Then Jamal made a great (**3. the middle of the outfield**) catch just inches away from the fence. Next up, Sean O'Malley (**4. made a one-base hit**) Fernandez to second. Then super-hitter Chuck Jordy sent the ball over the fence, bringing all the players on base home and bringing the team to victory.

5. What other baseball words do you know? Write them on the lines.

People	Places	Things
manager	bull pen	mitt
5.	7.	9.
6.	8.	10.

5. _____
6. _____
7. _____
8. _____
9. _____
10. _____

Name _____

WHAT'S IN A WORD?

Did you know that baseball, called America's greatest pastime, actually started in the 1400s as a game called Prisoner's Base? This game was named for the four bases that had to be touched in order to score. In England, people play a game called cricket that is similar to baseball but that has eleven players. There is a goal called a *wicket* at each end of the field instead of one home plate.

1. What sports do you like to play? List them and tell why you chose them.

HOMOPHONES Homophones are words that sound the same but have different spellings and meanings. Write the correct homophone for each clue.

bear/bare   hair/hare   stair/stare   there/they're

2. a kind of rabbit
3. a step
4. a word that means "they are"
5. without covering, or empty
6. something that isn't here
7. something you comb
8. a mammal that growls
9. to look at for a long time

PLAY A GUESSING GAME Work with a partner. Your partner acts out a Spelling Word without speaking. You try to guess the word and spell it. You get three chances. If you guess correctly, switch roles with your partner. Otherwise, have your partner act out another Spelling Word.

SPELLING WORDS

1. before
2. sport
3. store
4. form
5. war
6. warm
7. your
8. fort
9. story
10. wore
11. forth
12. force

Your Own Words

Look for other words with the vowel sound you hear in *your* to add to the lists. You might find *coral* and *shore* in a science article. Perhaps you will find *landform* or *north* in a social studies article.

13. _____
14. _____
15. _____

Words Like *your*

Each Spelling Word has the vowel sound you hear in *your*. Look at the letters that spell that sound.

Sort the Spelling Words in a way that will help you remember them. Three example words have been given. Fill in the last one as you are sorting.

▶ The vowel sound you hear in *your* can be spelled *or, ore, ar,* or *our.*

Name _____

Strategy Workshop

PROOFREADING: Checking Twice When you proofread, circle words you know are misspelled. Then proofread again. Look for words you are not sure of.

Proofread the list twice. Circle the misspelled words in each row. Then write the Spelling Words correctly.

1. fourt   warm
2. forse   your
3. before   spart
4. stor   story
5. wore   farth
6. war   fourm

1. _____
2. _____
3. _____
4. _____
5. _____
6. _____

7–11. Proofread this letter to Granny from the wolf twice. Circle the five words with spelling errors. Then write the Spelling Words correctly.

Dear Granny,
    Please read this befour you turn me in. I would not harm Red Riding Hood. I just wour yor clothes to keep worme. You must believe my stoury!
            Sincerely,
            Ilene Wolf

7. _____
8. _____
9. _____
10. _____
11. _____

FUN WITH WORDS Complete this cartoon with a Spelling Word.

What's the difference between __12__ and *warm*?

The letter *m*.

12. _____

Name _____

Vocabulary WordShop

Home Safety
WORDS

disguised
latch
knocked
pretended

SPELLING LOG Think about how you might use these words in your writing, and add them to your Spelling Log.

1. _____
2. _____
3. _____
4. _____

Use the Home Safety Words to complete this story.

"Please __1__ the door after I leave," said Mother. "And remember what I told you about strangers."

Mother forgot her key and __2__ on the door. Little Badger __3__ he wasn't home.

"Little Badger, it is Mother," she said. "Please let me in." But Little Badger knew that someone might be __4__ as Mother and did not let her in.

"We have taught Little Badger *too* well," said Mother.

WHAT'S IN A WORD?

In "Lon Po Po," Shang sees the wolf's *hairy* face. This puts Shang and her sisters in a *hairy* situation. *Hairy* used in this second way means "frightening, difficult, or exciting."

5. Tell about a *hairy* situation you have been in.

5. _____
_____
_____
_____
_____

Name _____

SLANG The word *hairy*, when used to describe something scary, is slang. Slang words are informal words that we use in everyday conversation. Sometimes slang words are new, and sometimes they are old words used in a new way.

Groovy was a slang word that meant "pleasing." Few people use the word now. Most slang words are used for only a short time.

Some slang words are used so often by so many people that they become Standard English. The words in the box used to be slang words.

| kids | skyscraper | jazz | cowlick |

Choose a word from the box to complete each sentence.
1. Those ___ are always up to something.
2. I love the sound of ___ music.
3. What's the tallest ___ in this city?
4. Your ___ is sticking up again!

5. What slang words do you use when you want to say that something is really great?
6. What other slang words do you know?

TRY IT OUT Climb up the word ladders. Start with the Spelling Word at the bottom. At each step, follow the directions to make another Spelling Word.

```
                    12. – c           b e _ _ _ _

                    11. – m + ce      _ _ _ _ _

8. + m _ _ _ _      10. – t + m       _ _ _ _

7. – ore + ar _ _ _  9. – h           _ _ _ _

wore                forth
```

1. _____
2. _____
3. _____
4. _____
5. _____
6. _____
7. _____
8. _____
9. _____
10. _____
11. _____
12. _____

Integrated Spelling   LESSON 15   69

Name _____

Homophones

SPELLING WORDS

1. one
2. here
3. hear
4. won
5. eight
6. hour
7. our
8. ate
9. seen
10. blue
11. scene
12. blew

Each Spelling Word is a homophone. Homophones are words that sound the same but have different meanings and spellings. Think about meaning as you look at the way each homophone is spelled.

Sort the Spelling Words into pairs of homophones to help you remember them.

Your Own Words

Look for other homophones to add to the lists. You might find *rain* in a science book, *reign* in a social studies book, and *rein* in an article about horses.

13. _____
14. _____
15. _____

▶ **Homophones are words that sound the same but have different meanings and spellings.**

Name _____

Strategy Workshop

PROOFREADING: Reading for Meaning

When you proofread, look for homophones. Make sure that each word you have written makes sense in the sentence. Sometimes you can make up a clue to help you remember the meaning of a word. For example: You *hear* with your *ears*.

Write the Spelling Word for each clue.

1. past tense of *win*   2. number between seven and nine
3. belonging to us

4–11. Here is a news report from the brick house of the third little pig. Draw a line under the words that make sense, and write them on the lines.

Good News! At this (4. hour, our) we (5. hear, here) that the Three Little Pigs have built their houses.
Bad News! The wolf has blown down (6. won, one) of the houses.
Good News! The first pig has been (7. scene, seen) at the stick house with his brother.
Bad News! The wolf (8. blew, blue) down the stick house.
Good News! The pigs have joined us (9. here, hear) at the brick house.
Bad News! The wolf has arrived at this (10. scene, seen).
Good News! The pigs (11. eight, ate) wolf stew for dinner.

FUN WITH WORDS Use a Spelling Word that names a color to complete the cartoon.

1. _____
2. _____
3. _____

4. _____
5. _____
6. _____
7. _____
8. _____
9. _____
10. _____
11. _____

12. _____

Name _____

Desert WORDS

- southwestern
- cactus
- dust storm
- adobe

SPELLING LOG Think about how you might use these words in your writing, and add them to your Spelling Log.

1. _____
2. _____
3. _____
4. _____

5. _____
_____
_____
_____

Vocabulary WordShop

Use the Desert Words to complete the postcard message.

Dear Joey,
    We are in Arizona now. It's in the **1** part of the country. We are staying in a house made of mud. It is called an **2** house. A **3** with fruit is growing right outside our door. Last night we saw a **4**. You wouldn't believe the clouds of dust that blew by! See you next month.

    Your traveling friend,
    Tucker

Joey Lamott
234 Angel Street
Milford, NH
03768

WHAT'S IN A WORD?

Have your parents ever told you not to make a scene? The word *scene* used in this way means "a show of strong feeling." But *scene* can also mean "a view," "a part of a performance in a play or movie," or "the place where something happens," such as the *scene* of a crime. The word *scene* comes from the Greek word *skene*, which means "stage" or "tent."

5. How is a stage or a tent related to a performance? Write your ideas on the lines.

Name _____

DICTIONARY In a dictionary, the sentence following a definition gives an example of how an entry word is used. Some words have more than one definition and more than one example sentence.

hear [hir] *v.* **1.** to get sound through the ears; to sense with the ears: **I can *hear* the neighbors' phone ringing when their window is open. 2.** to know or find out about: **Did you ever *hear* of a ship called the *Titanic*?**

Which definition of *hear* is used in each sentence? Write the meaning on an answer line.

1. When will you *hear* if you made the team?
2. I would like to *hear* that music again.

DESCRIBING WORDS Write a describing word from the box to complete the details about the cactus.

| prickly | egg-shaped | wide | white |

3. massive, _____ trunk
4. waxy, _____ flowers
5. ripe, _____ fruit
6. long, _____ spines

1. _____
   _____
   _____
2. _____
   _____
   _____
3. _____
4. _____
5. _____
6. _____

WRITE A SILLY STORY Work with a classmate. Write the first sentence of the story, using one Spelling Word. Have your partner write the second sentence, using another Spelling Word. Take turns until you have used as many of the Spelling Words as possible.

Integrated Spelling

LESSON 16   73

Name _____

Calendar Words

SPELLING WORDS

1. May
2. Sunday
3. June
4. July
5. date
6. winter
7. year
8. Friday
9. March
10. Monday
11. April
12. summer

Each Spelling Word is a calendar word.

Sort the Spelling Words in a way that will help you remember them.

Look for other calendar words to add to the lists. You will probably find *autumn* and *spring* in a science book. You might find *days* and *weeks* in your math book.

13. _____
14. _____
15. _____

▶ The names of months and days are capitalized. The names of seasons and some other calendar words are not capitalized.

74 LESSON 17

Integrated Spelling

Name _____

Strategy Workshop

PROOFREADING: Reading Backward When you proofread, read slowly. Start with the last word and end with the first. Then read for meaning.

Proofread from right to left, and circle the spelling errors in each row. Then write the correct spellings.

1.	summer	Munday	June	July
2–3.	date	wintur	yair	Friday
4–5.	Marth	Sunday	April	Mai

6–11. Proofread the club notes. Go from the last word to the first. Circle the six spelling errors. Then read for meaning, and write the correct spellings.

1. _____
2. _____
3. _____
4. _____
5. _____

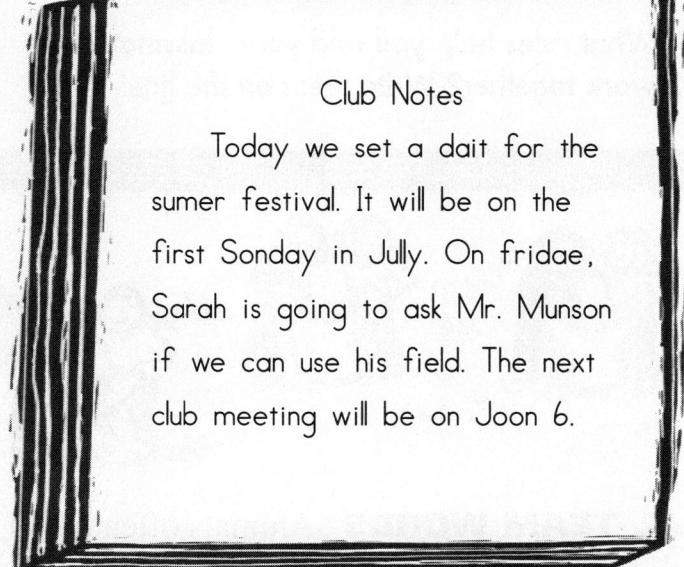

Club Notes
Today we set a dait for the sumer festival. It will be on the first Sonday in Jully. On fridae, Sarah is going to ask Mr. Munson if we can use his field. The next club meeting will be on Joon 6.

6. _____
7. _____
8. _____
9. _____
10. _____
11. _____

FUN WITH WORDS Complete this familiar expression with a Spelling Word.

12. _____ showers bring May flowers.

12. _____

Integrated Spelling · LESSON 17

Name _____

Team WORDS

together
partner
cooperate
connects

SPELLING LOG Think about how you might use these words in your writing, and add them to your Spelling Log.

1. _____
2. _____
3. _____
4. _____
5. _____
_____
_____
_____

Vocabulary WordShop

Use the Team Words to complete these directions for planning a school field day. Match one word for each number.

Plan a Field Day

1. Share your idea with a _____.
2. _____ by taking turns and listening carefully.
3. Find out how your idea _____ with the ideas of your classmates.
4. Work _____ to make your field day a big success!
5. What rules help you and your classmates work together? Write them on the lines.

ANIMAL TEAM WORDS Animals often travel and work together in groups for survival. Our language has words that name these groups. For instance, we call a group of wolves a *pack*.

Write the name of the group each animal travels in. If you need help, look it up in a thesaurus or encyclopedia.

6. A group of bees
7. A group of sheep
8. A group of lions
9. A group of fish
10. A group of cattle
11. A group of geese

6. _____
7. _____
8. _____
9. _____
10. _____
11. _____

Name _____

WHAT'S IN A WORD?

Frya was the Norse goddess of love. It is said that when she was happy, the sky was full of colors. *Friday*, a day of the week, is named after Frya. In Old English, this day was spelled *Frigedaeg*.

1. What is your favorite day of the week? Write it on the line and tell why you chose it.

PROPER NOUNS Some nouns name specific persons, places, or things. These are called *proper nouns*. For instance, *month* is a noun, but *July* is a proper noun. Proper nouns are always capitalized.

2–9. Beverly Cleary is the author of many books for children, including *Ramona Quimby, Age 8*. Read the letter to Beverly Cleary. Circle the proper nouns. Then write them on the lines. Use capital letters where they are needed.

june 13

Dear Mrs. cleary,
    I love reading your books. I live on a street just like klickitat street, and I'm a lot like ramona. At least that's what my teacher, Miss warner, says about me. Will you send me a card for my birthday? It's on july 8.
            Your friend,
            samantha

WITH A PARTNER Choose a Spelling Word. On a sheet of paper, draw a blank for each letter in the word. Ask a classmate to guess a letter. If the letter is in your word, write it on the correct blank. If the letter is not in the word, write it at one side. Continue playing until your partner guesses the word. Then switch places.

1. _____
   _____
   _____
   _____
   _____
   _____

2. _____
3. _____
4. _____
5. _____
6. _____
7. _____
8. _____
9. _____

Integrated Spelling   LESSON 17   77

Name _____

Practice Test

A. Read each sentence. Is the spelling of the underlined word correct or incorrect? Mark the answer sheet.

Example: We built a <u>brown</u> boat.
　　correct　　incorrect

1. We <u>enjoy</u> playing together.
　　correct　　incorrect

2. Do you want to use my <u>oyl</u> paints?
　　correct　　incorrect

3. What a <u>lowd</u> noise they are making!
　　correct　　incorrect

4. They made a <u>large</u> banner.
　　correct　　incorrect

5. What do you want to <u>wear</u> as a uniform?
　　correct　　incorrect

6. It's not polite to <u>stayr</u>.
　　correct　　incorrect

7. What do you see over <u>there</u>?
　　correct　　incorrect

8. Let's build a <u>fourt</u>!
　　correct　　incorrect

9. We ate <u>befor</u> we left.
　　correct　　incorrect

10. I really like <u>your</u> idea.
　　correct　　incorrect

EXAMPLE
● correct ○ incorrect

ANSWERS
1. ○ correct ○ incorrect
2. ○ correct ○ incorrect
3. ○ correct ○ incorrect
4. ○ correct ○ incorrect
5. ○ correct ○ incorrect
6. ○ correct ○ incorrect
7. ○ correct ○ incorrect
8. ○ correct ○ incorrect
9. ○ correct ○ incorrect
10. ○ correct ○ incorrect

Name _____

B. Read each sentence. Is the spelling of the underlined word correct or incorrect? Mark the answer sheet.

1. Let's go in and get <u>wurm</u>.
   correct   incorrect

2. <u>Eght</u> people are coming to help.
   correct   incorrect

3. The wind <u>blew</u> down our tree house.
   correct   incorrect

4. We can go in one <u>huor</u>.
   correct   incorrect

5. Have you <u>seen</u> the other team?
   correct   incorrect

6. <u>Wenter</u> is my favorite season.
   correct   incorrect

7. Who has a birthday in <u>June</u>?
   correct   incorrect

8. Our first lesson is on <u>Monday</u>.
   correct   incorrect

9. I will be old enough next <u>yair</u>.
   correct   incorrect

10. Let's play over <u>heer</u>.
    correct   incorrect

ANSWERS

1. ◯ correct   ◯ incorrect
2. ◯ correct   ◯ incorrect
3. ◯ correct   ◯ incorrect
4. ◯ correct   ◯ incorrect
5. ◯ correct   ◯ incorrect
6. ◯ correct   ◯ incorrect
7. ◯ correct   ◯ incorrect
8. ◯ correct   ◯ incorrect
9. ◯ correct   ◯ incorrect
10. ◯ correct   ◯ incorrect

Integrated Spelling   **LESSON 18 • REVIEW**

Unit 3: Writing Activities

WORDS TO WATCH FOR

enjoyed
everywhere
held
hitting
find
lady
sea
toward

Step into Action!

With a group of classmates, think of things you can do to improve your neighborhood. Perhaps you can find an area that needs to be cleaned, such as a beach or park area. How can you convince others that your plan is a good one? Write a persuasive letter to all the students in your school. Convince them that your goal is important. Include all five parts of a letter. Deliver the letter. When they are convinced, get them to help!

Tips for Spelling Success

- You want the person who is reading your letter to concentrate on your ideas and not on your spelling.
- Proofread your letter twice.
- Correct misspelled words.
- On the left are some Words to Watch For.
- Look in your Spelling Log for words to help you express how strongly you feel about your goal. These emotional words may help convince your reader.

Tips for Spelling Success

- Make sure you write your suggestions clearly and completely.
- You might want to write a word several ways, compare spellings, and choose the one that looks right to you.
- Look up the word in a dictionary if you are still not sure how to spell it.

Let's Work Together

Think of a time when you worked with a group and the work went well. Make a class chart that lists suggestions for ways to work well with other people. Hang the list on your classroom bulletin board as a reminder to everyone.

Name _____

Awesome Authors

Who is your favorite author? Make a chart that lists the author's books or stories you have read and tells a little about each one. Add to the chart as you read other books by the author. Post the chart where others can see it. Perhaps you'll find other classmates who like this author, too. If so, you may want to get together to talk about the author's books.

Tips for Spelling Success
- When you proofread your chart, look for words that sound like other words.
- Think about the meaning of the word you want to use, and make sure you have used the correct spelling of the word.

Catchy Categories

Complete the category chart. Write a word that fits each category and begins with the letter on the left. A few of the boxes have been filled in for you.

Tips for Spelling Success
- If you are not sure how to spell a word while completing the chart, spell the word the way it sounds.
- When you have finished the activity, look up the word in a dictionary and correct any misspellings.

	Animal	Place	Color	Thing
B	bear	_____	brown	bread
E	_____	_____	_____	_____
S	_____	store	_____	_____
T	_____	_____	_____	_____

Integrated Spelling

Name ____________________

Words Like *her*

SPELLING WORDS

1. girl
2. fur
3. her
4. bird
5. word
6. person
7. first
8. turn
9. third
10. hurt
11. church
12. work

Each Spelling Word has the vowel sound you hear in *her*. Look at the letters that spell that sound.

Sort the Spelling Words in a way that will help you remember them. Three example words have been given. Fill in the last one as you are sorting.

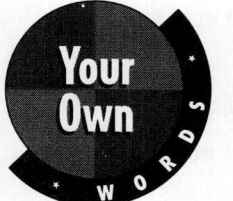

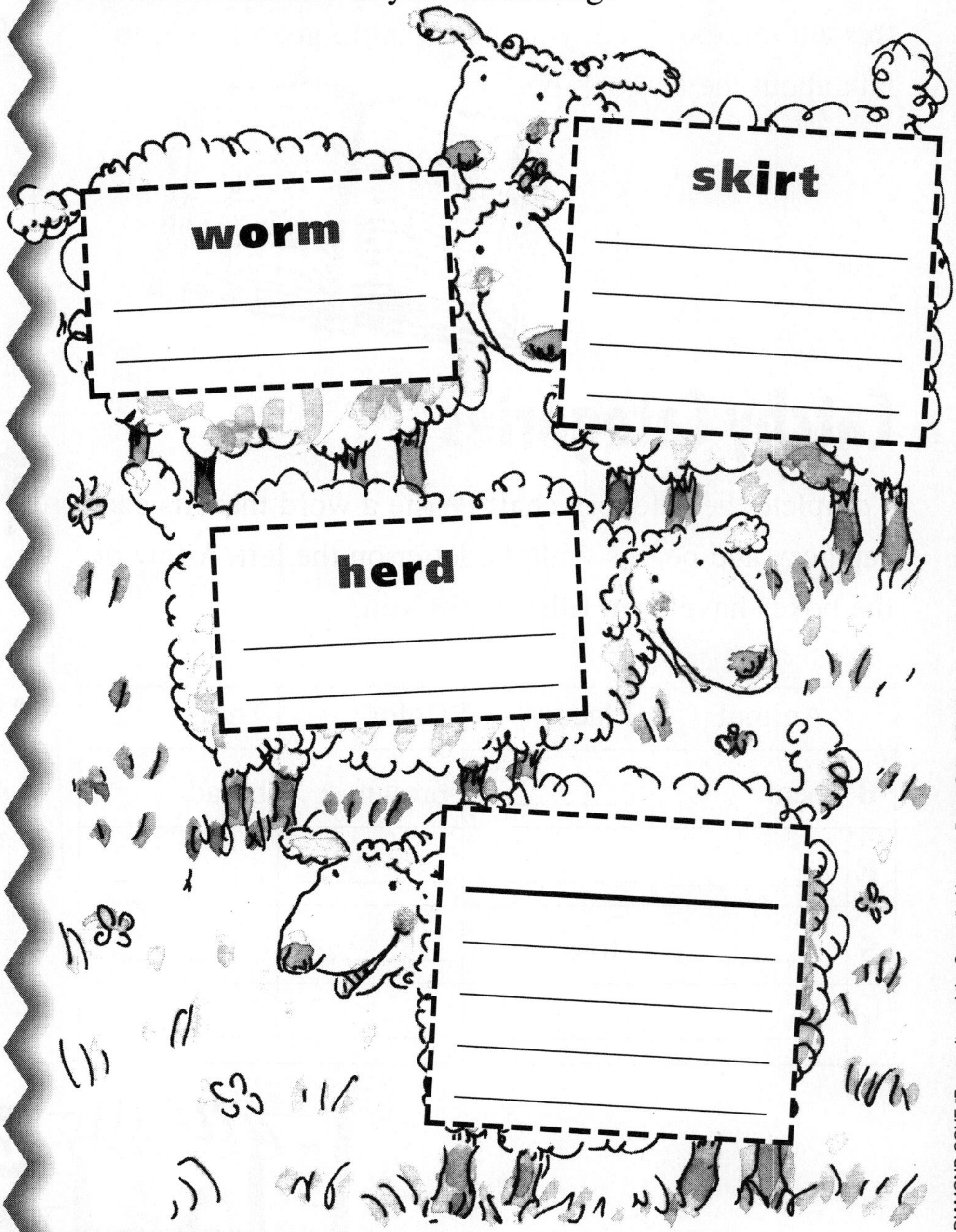

worm
skirt
herd

▶ **The vowel sound you hear in *her* can be spelled *ir*, *er*, *or*, or *ur*.**

Your Own WORDS

Look for other words like *her* to add to the lists. In a sports story, you might find *twirl* or *serve*. In a cookbook, you might find *turnip* or *burn*.

13. ____________________
14. ____________________
15. ____________________

Name _____

Strategy Workshop

PROOFREADING: Using a Dictionary After spelling a word, look at it carefully. If you are not sure whether it is spelled correctly, check in the dictionary.

Look at each word below. Decide whether it is spelled correctly. If you need help, use the Spelling Dictionary. Then write each word correctly.

1. hir
2. cherch
3. tern
4. werd
5. gurl

6–10. Read the letter below. Circle each word that is spelled wrong. Then write each word correctly.

Dear Aunt Fluffy,
 A coyote tried to eat me, but I was not hert. I furst fooled him by saying I must get fatter. Then I made him jump in a pond, and his fer got all wet! The thord time he came by, I also got away. Tricking a coyote is hard wirk, but I like it!
  Your little lamb,
  Borreguita

WORKING WITH MEANING Write Spelling Words to replace numbers 11 and 12.

I wish I were a **11**, so I could fly.

I wish I were a **12**, so I could talk!

1. _____
2. _____
3. _____
4. _____
5. _____

6. _____
7. _____
8. _____
9. _____
10. _____

11. _____
12. _____

Integrated Spelling LESSON 19

Prairie
WORDS

clover
field
meadow
thicket

SPELLING LOG Think about how you might use these words in your writing, and add them to your Spelling Log.

1. _____
2. _____
3. _____
4. _____

5. _____
6. _____
7. _____
8. _____

Vocabulary WordShop

Help the lamb find its way through the prairie. Replace each numbered item with a Prairie Word. The clues below will help you.

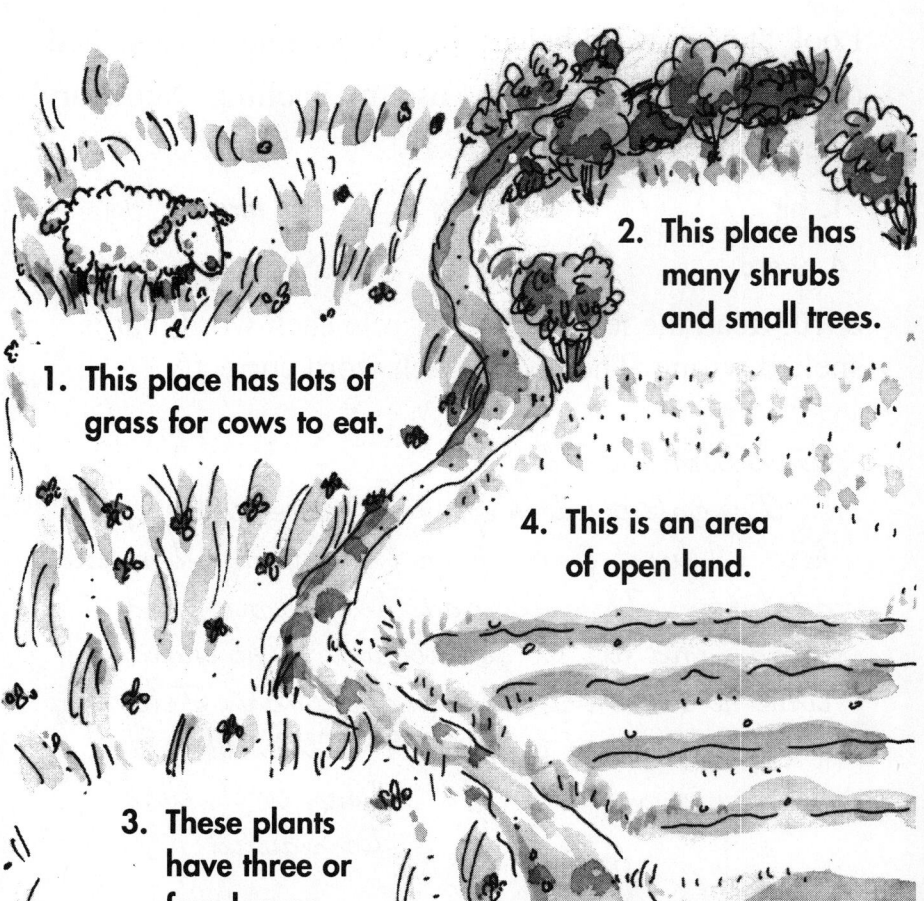

1. This place has lots of grass for cows to eat.
2. This place has many shrubs and small trees.
3. These plants have three or four leaves.
4. This is an area of open land.

5–8. Write other words about prairies that you know.

Name _____

WHAT'S IN A WORD?

The word *prairie* comes from the Latin word *pratum*, meaning "meadow." A prairie, like a meadow, is a large area of grassy land. *Prairie* and *meadow* are synonyms, or words with similar meanings.

1. Write another Prairie Word that is a synonym for *prairie* and *meadow*.

SYNONYMS In the field, find the word that is a synonym for each underlined word below. Write each word.

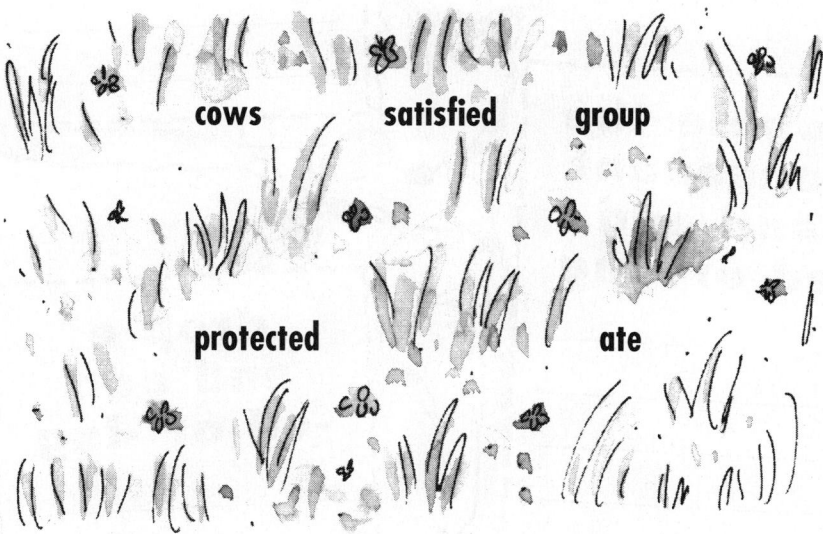

cows   satisfied   group

protected   ate

2. A <u>herd</u> of cows went to the field.
3. The <u>cattle</u> ate the sweet grass.
4. The cows <u>grazed</u> quietly all day.
5. A cowboy <u>guarded</u> the cows.
6. They ate until they were <u>full</u>.

1. _____
2. _____
3. _____
4. _____
5. _____
6. _____

MAKE A MATCH Work with a partner. Write each Spelling Word on an index card. Write a synonym for each word on another index card. See if your partner can match each Spelling Word with its synonym.

Integrated Spelling   LESSON 19   85

SPELLING WORDS

1. wagging
2. saved
3. taking
4. hopped
5. having
6. pulled
7. picked
8. letting
9. running
10. shopped
11. moved
12. coming

Look for other words that end with *-ed* or *-ing* to add to the lists. On a road sign, you might find *crossing* or *falling*. In your math book, you might find *divided* or *sharing*.

13. _____
14. _____
15. _____

Words That End with -ed and -ing

Each Spelling Word ends with *-ed* or *-ing*. Look for changes in the spelling of the base word when these endings are added.

Sort the Spelling Words in a way that will help you remember them.

- add -ed or -ing
- double the consonant and add -ed or -ing
- drop e and add -ed or -ing

▶ If a word ends in a vowel and consonant, double the consonant and add *-ed* or *-ing*.
▶ If a word ends in two consonants, just add *-ed* or *-ing*.
▶ If a word ends in a consonant and *e*, drop the *e* and add *-ed* or *-ing*.

Name _____

Strategy Workshop

PROOFREADING: Word Parts When you proofread, pay attention to word endings. Did you make the correct spelling changes before adding *-ed* or *-ing*?

Add the ending and write a Spelling Word.

1. shop + ed
2. pull + ed
3. have + ing
4. save + ed
5. let + ing
6. take + ing

7–11. Proofread the poem. Be sure to check word endings. Circle the spelling errors, and write the words correctly.

A wolf was runing through the woods.
It hoppd upon a log.
First all I saw was its waging tail
So I thought it was a dog!
But then it moveed and turned around,
And I could plainly tell.
The wolf pickked up its head and howled
A very wolflike yell!

FUN WITH WORDS Follow the directions to write a Spelling Word.

12.  + ing − b =

1. _____
2. _____
3. _____
4. _____
5. _____
6. _____

7. _____
8. _____
9. _____
10. _____
11. _____

12. _____

Integrated Spelling

Wolf WORDS

territory
boundaries
attacks
prey

SPELLING LOG Think about how you might use these words in your writing, and add them to your Spelling Log.

1. _____
2. _____
3. _____
4. _____

Vocabulary WordShop

Wolves would like people to know a few things. You can help. Replace each number with one of the Wolf Words.

Wolf Talk

We are peaceful animals. If no one _1_ us, we will not come after you.

Our _2_ is our home. Please do not threaten or chase us on our own land.

Don't think of us as cruel when we hunt our _3_ . Remember, we don't have supermarkets to shop in!

We don't mind fences to mark the _4_ of our land. After all, good fences make good neighbors.

5–8. Write other words about wolves.

5. _____
6. _____
7. _____
8. _____

Name _____

WHAT'S IN A WORD?

There are many sayings that contain the word *wolf*. For example, *to cry wolf* means "to give a false alarm." It comes from a story about a boy who cried "Wolf!" as a joke, so that people would run to help him. Later, a wolf really did come. But no one answered the boy's cries then, because those who heard him didn't believe him.

1. What do you think the saying "wolf in sheep's clothing" means?
2. What do you think the saying "to wolf down your food" means?

ANIMAL SAYINGS Choose a word from the box to finish each saying.

| stubborn | busy | happy | sly | slippery |

3. The fox is known as a very sneaky animal. A sneaky person is said to be "as _____ as a fox."
4. A mule will not move when it doesn't want to. A person who must have his or her own way is said to be "as _____ as a mule."
5. The eel is a fish that is hard to catch. Someone who gets away quickly is said to be "as _____ as an eel."
6. A beaver is known for always working. Someone who works all the time is said to be "as _____ as a beaver."
7. The lark is a cheerful bird. A cheerful person is said to be "as _____ as a lark."

ACT IT OUT Work with a partner. Play a guessing game with the Spelling Words. One partner acts out one of the words without speaking. The other partner guesses the word and spells it. Then the partners switch roles.

Integrated Spelling

1. _____
_____
_____
_____
_____
_____
_____

2. _____
_____
_____
_____
_____
_____
_____

3. _____
4. _____
5. _____
6. _____
7. _____

Words Like *ago* **and** *begin*

SPELLING WORDS

1. alone
2. below
3. along
4. ago
5. behind
6. begin
7. asleep
8. again
9. ahead
10. become
11. above
12. besides

Look for other words like *ago* and *begin* to add to the lists. You may find *beyond* or *aboard* in a movie title.

13. _____
14. _____
15. _____

Each Spelling Word begins with *a* or *be*. In each word the stress falls on the second syllable.

Sort the Spelling Words in a way that will help you remember them. One example word is given. Fill in the other one as you are sorting.

around

▶ Many words begin with *a* or *be*. In most of them, the stress falls on the second syllable.

Name _____

Strategy Workshop

SPELLING CLUES: Choosing the Right Letters As you write Spelling Words to complete the story below, check the placement of each letter.

"Look, Jason," said Lola. "Ginny is painting the sign for the recreation center. She is working all _1_."

"Let's help her," said Jason. Jason ran toward Ginny, and Lola ran _2_ him.

Lola took a large brush and painted up _3_ her head. Jason helped Ginny finish the red edge down _4_ the letters.

"Thanks," said Ginny as she passed _5_ the paint pan. "I should have had this sign finished two days _6_."

Look at each pair of words below and circle the word that is misspelled. Then write the correct word.

1. _____
2. _____
3. _____
4. _____
5. _____
6. _____

7. again / agin
8. besides / bessides
9. beggin / begin
10. asleep / asleepe

7. _____
8. _____
9. _____
10. _____

FUN WITH WORDS Write a Spelling Word to solve each word-and-picture puzzle.

11. 🐝 + come =

12. a + 👦 =

11. _____
12. _____

Integrated Spelling   LESSON 21   **91**

Animal
WORDS

mammal
reptiles
amphibians
rodent

SPELLING LOG Think about how you might use these words in your writing, and add them to your Spelling Log.

1. _____
2. _____
3. _____
4. _____

5. _____
6. _____
7. _____
8. _____

Name _____

Vocabulary WordShop

Here are four signs you might find at the zoo to tell about where different animals live. Complete each sign by writing an Animal Word. The underlined letter clues may help you.

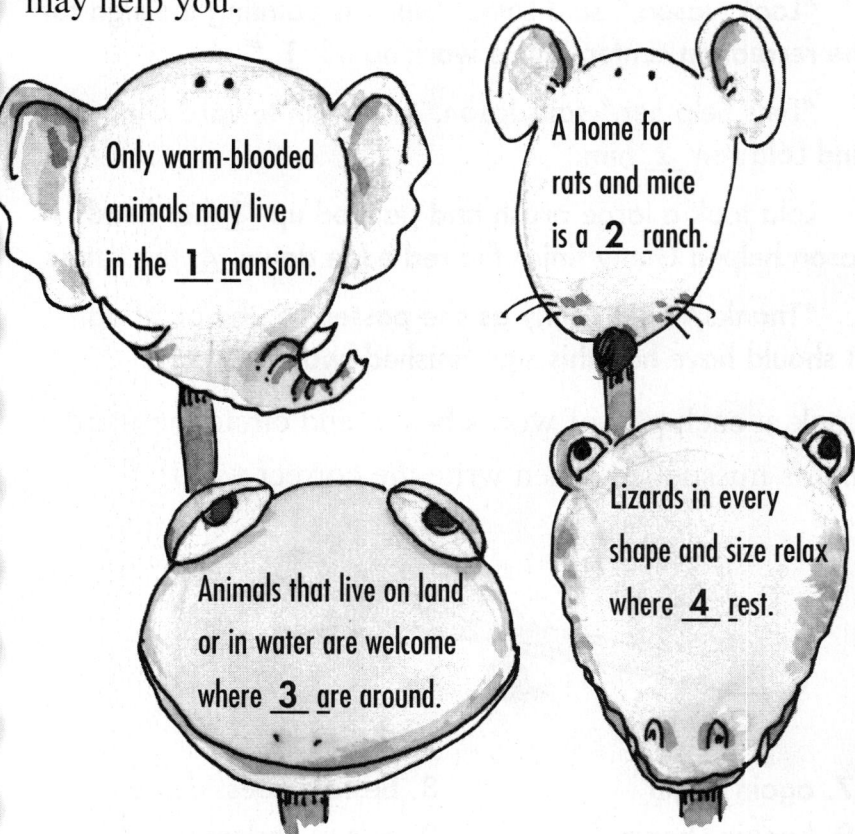

Only warm-blooded animals may live in the **1** mansion.

A home for rats and mice is a **2** ranch.

Animals that live on land or in water are welcome where **3** are around.

Lizards in every shape and size relax where **4** rest.

5–8. Write other words to describe these two areas for animals at the zoo.

Name _____

WHAT'S IN A WORD?

Some dictionaries identify animals and plants by their Latin as well as their English names. For example, the official Latin name for the cardinal (the bird) is *cardinalis*.

Look at the Latin animal names below, and write the English name of each one. Use a dictionary for help.

1. cattus   2. bufalus

SOUND-ALIKES Work with a partner to write a Spelling Word that rhymes with each of these terms.

3. find   4. bed   5. rides
6. song   7. love   8. cone

SAY AND WRITE Say these Spelling Words and have a partner write them on a sheet of paper. Then switch roles and write the words as your partner pronounces them. Finally, write the words on the lines.

9. again   10. below   11. ago
12. become 13. begin   14. asleep

1. _____
2. _____
3. _____
4. _____
5. _____
6. _____
7. _____
8. _____

9. _____
10. _____
11. _____
12. _____
13. _____
14. _____

Integrated Spelling

Name _____

Contractions and Possessives

SPELLING WORDS

1. boy's
2. I'd
3. we've
4. what's
5. girl's
6. he'd
7. its
8. it's
9. teacher's
10. they've
11. she'd
12. giant's

Each Spelling Word is a contraction or a possessive. Look for an apostrophe (') in most of the words.

Sort the Spelling Words in a way that will help you remember them. One example word is given. Fill in the other one as you are sorting.

I'm

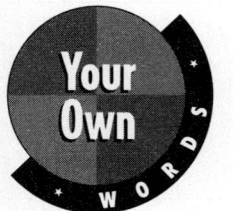

Look for other contractions and possessives to add to the lists. Read a comic strip, and look for characters saying words like *Mom's* or *I'm*.

13. _____
14. _____
15. _____

▶ A contraction is a short way to write two words. An apostrophe replaces any missing letters.
▶ A possessive shows ownership. It may end in 's. The possessive *its* does not have an apostrophe.

Name _____

Strategy Workshop

SPELLING CLUES: Contractions and Possessives Think about contractions, the short way to write a word or group of words. Use an apostrophe (') to replace the letter or letters you have to leave out. To write a possessive, you usually add *'s*. The possessive *its* does not have an apostrophe.

Write a contraction for each pair of words.

1. he would   2. they have   3. what is

Add *'s* to show ownership. Write the possessive of these words.

4. boy   5. teacher   6. giant

7–11. Circle the five misspelled words in Tom's hasty note to his mother. Then write each word correctly.

Mom,
A spider has spun its' web near the pond. Its still light enough outside to take a snapshot. I'd like to if we've got any film. Latasha said shed go along. May I go?
— Tom

FUN WITH WORDS Write the possessive word correctly.

12. A girlz curls

1. _____
2. _____
3. _____

4. _____
5. _____
6. _____

7. _____
8. _____
9. _____
10. _____
11. _____

12. _____

Integrated Spelling   LESSON 22

Pond Life WORDS

clings
glides
skim
swoop

SPELLING LOG Think about how you might use these words in your writing and add them to your Spelling Log.

1. _____
2. _____
3. _____
4. _____

5. _____
6. _____
7. _____

8. _____
9. _____
10. _____

11. _____

Vocabulary WordShop

Use a Pond Life Word to complete each caption.

1. Water ____ to the duck's bill.

2. Its webbed feet ____ the surface as the duck flaps its wings.

3. Diving birds ____ down on dragonflies.

4. In the deep end of the pond, a swan ____.

5–7. Write the names of other creatures or actions you might see around a pond.

WHAT'S IN A WORD?

The dictionary lists *cattail* among words that begin with *cat*, such as *catkin* and *cat's-eye*.

Match each of the cat words from the box with its correct definition below.

| cat's cradle | catnap | catnip |

8. a short sleep   9. a minty herb   10. a string game
11. Name another word or phrase that begins with *cat*.

96 LESSON 22

Integrated Spelling

Name _____

1–6. CONTRACTION SCRAMBLE Write each word from the box on a separate index card. Mix up the cards and place them face down. With a classmate, take turns flipping over two cards at a time. If the two cards can make a contraction, read the two words. Then say, spell, and write the contraction they make. If the two words do not make a contraction, turn the cards face down again.

1. _____
2. _____
3. _____
4. _____
5. _____
6. _____

```
I   would   we   have   what   is   he   they   she
```

FLASH CARDS Divide the Spelling Words equally with a partner. Make a flash card for each of your six Spelling Words, and write a sentence using that word. Underline the word. Here are two sample sentences:

<u>It's</u> a great day for skipping stones on the pond.
The goose spread <u>its</u> wings as it flew into the sky.

Taking turns, say each Spelling Word, read its sentence, and ask your partner to write the word on the board. Use your flash card to check your partner's spelling.

Integrated Spelling   LESSON 22   97

SPELLING WORDS

1. baby's
2. boys'
3. mother's
4. men's
5. brother's
6. kids'
7. sisters'
8. father's
9. dog's
10. teachers'
11. class's
12. babies'

Look for other possessives to add to the lists. Read labels and box tops to look for words like *cook's* and *family's*.

13. _____
14. _____
15. _____

More Possessives

Each Spelling Word is a possessive. If the word names one person or thing, add *'s* to make the word possessive. If the word names more than one person or thing and ends with *s*, add an *'* to make the word possessive.

Sort the Spelling Words in a way that will help you remember them. Two example words have been given.

▶ To form the possessive of a word that names one person or thing, add *'s*: *the baby's bottle*.

▶ If the word names more than one and already ends in *s*, just add *'*: *the babies' bottles*.

▶ If the word names more than one and does not end in *s*, add *'s*: *the men's jobs*.

Name _____

Strategy Workshop

SPELLING CLUES: Possessives To write a possessive, think of how the word is spelled, and then add an apostrophe or an apostrophe and *s*.

girl ⟶ girl's | girls ⟶ girls'

Follow the wheels of this prairie wagon by making each word plural, and then plural and possessive.

1. kid ⟶ kids ⟶
2. baby ⟶ babies ⟶
3. teacher ⟶ teachers ⟶
4. boy ⟶ boys ⟶

Think of the possessive endings for the words in parentheses. Then write the complete words on the lines.

5. one (baby) swing
6. Sandra's (mother) skillet
7. my (brother) bucket handle
8. the music (class) triangle
9. four (sister) bed frames
10. six (men) watch chains
11. my (father) saddle
12. April's (dog) collar buckle

1. _____
2. _____
3. _____
4. _____

5. _____
6. _____
7. _____
8. _____
9. _____
10. _____
11. _____
12. _____

Integrated Spelling

Nature
WORDS

wildlife
vegetation
predator
inhabit

SPELLING LOG Think about how you might use these words in your writing, and add them to your Spelling Log.

1. _____
2. _____
3. _____
4. _____

5. _____
6. _____
7. _____
8. _____

Name _____

Vocabulary WordShop

Look at the picture postcard below of a scene from the Rocky Mountains. Then use the Nature Words to complete this diary entry describing a trip out West.

August 5

Dear Diary,
Along the way, we studied a huge green cactus and other __1__. I saw many __2__, such as rabbits, lizards, and birds. My father said that the vulture overhead is a __3__. It is one of the many birds that __4__ the open prairie and circle the blue sky. I wonder what we'll see tomorrow!

5–8. Write other words that describe things you might see on a nature walk.

Name _____

WHAT'S IN A WORD?

Did you know that the word *alligator* comes from the Spanish *el lagarto*, which means "the lizard"? The word first appeared in English in 1568 as "a monstrous *Lagarto*." Shakespeare spelled it *Allegater* in 1623. Words can change over time, in spelling and pronunciation.

1. Name two other reptiles that can be called *the lizard*. (*el lagarto*)

1. _____
   _____
   _____

WHOSE IS IT? The chart below is incomplete. On the lines, write Spelling Words to supply the missing words in each column.

Singular		Plural	
bird	bird's	birds	birds'
2. baby	____	____	____
3. brother	____	brothers	brothers'
4. mother	____	mothers	mothers'
5. boy	boy's	____	____
6. teacher	teacher's	____	____

2. _____
   _____
   _____
   _____
3. _____
4. _____
5. _____
6. _____
   _____

FUN WITH A GROUP Choose one person to be "it" for your group. As a group, spell aloud the possessives of these words. When you get to the apostrophe, the person who is "it" stands up and says "apostrophe."

7. kids
8. dog
9. father
10. men
11. class
12. sisters

7. _____
8. _____
9. _____
10. _____
11. _____
12. _____

Integrated Spelling

Name _____

Practice Test

A. Read each sentence. Find the correctly spelled word to complete each sentence. On the answer sheet, mark the letter next to that word.

Example:
  One ____ in my family likes nature movies.
  A purson   B pirson   C person

1. The ____ on a coyote is smooth.
   A fer   B fur   C furr

2. Which bird ____ on the first limb?
   A hopped   B hopt   C hopd

3. My ____ hobby is painting wildlife.
   A fathers   B father's   C fathe'rs

4. Raccoon tracks were seen ____ the waterfall.
   A bleow   B be-low   C below

5. A wolf was ____ across the open prairie.
   A running   B runing   C runeing

6. The meadow was ____ territory.
   A it's   B its   C its'

7. My two ____ wildflower collections are their treasures.
   A sisters   B sisters'   C siste'rs

8. We could see clover ____.
   A ahead   B a-head   C ahhead

9. A dragonfly ____ away from the rocks.
   A movied   B moveed   C moved

10. ____ been studying the wolf's habitat.
    A Weve   B We'ave   C We've

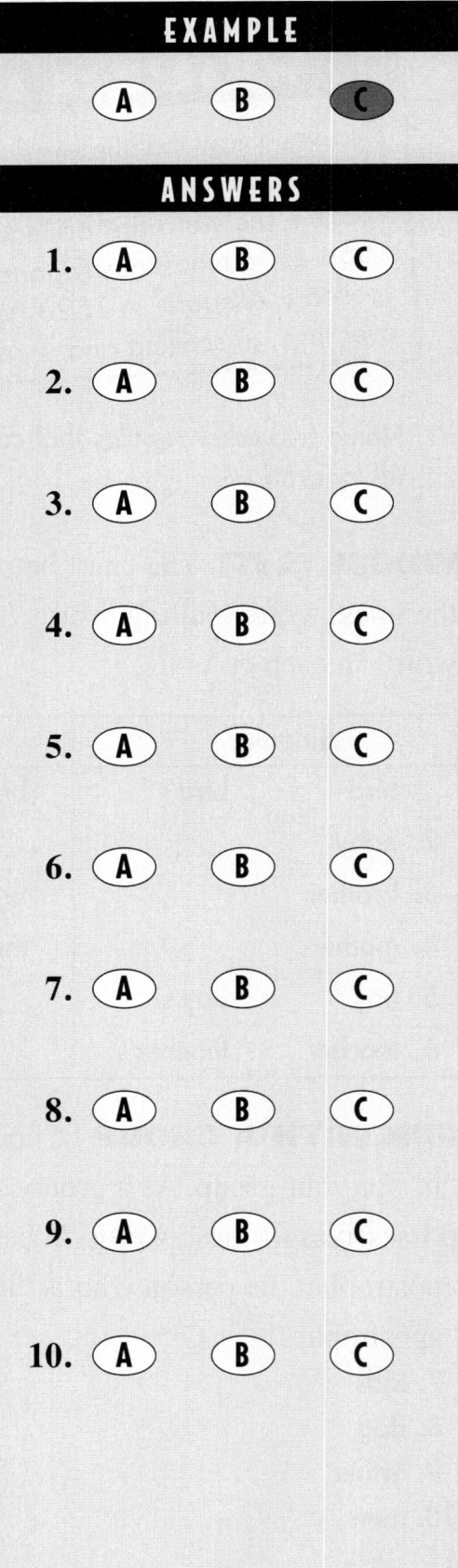

102 LESSON 24 • REVIEW   Integrated Spelling

Name _____

B. Read each sentence. Find the correctly spelled word to complete each sentence. On the answer sheet, mark the letter next to that word.

1. ____ the way to the pond, the owl swooped into a thicket.
   A Allong   B A-long   C Along

2. Marta is ____ the fish loose in the water.
   A letting   B leting   C leteing

3. Behind the ____ house grew a field of daisies.
   A dog's   B dogs   C do'gs

4. The ____ names for their rodents were Ratman and Mickey.
   A boys   B boys'   C bo'ys

5. The reptile's prey escaped and was not ____.
   A hirt   B hert   C hurt

6. A dandelion ____ the hut spread its seeds.
   A behind   B beehind   C be-hind

7. Our playing field looks like a ____ footprint.
   A giants   B giant's   C giants'

8. Water glides down the side of the canyon from the rocks ____.
   A above   B abbove   C a-bove

9. The dog stood ____ its tail at the field mouse.
   A wageing   B wagng   C wagging

10. Edward and his brother ____ two names for the bat.
    A picked   B piced   C pickked

ANSWERS

1. A B C
2. A B C
3. A B C
4. A B C
5. A B C
6. A B C
7. A B C
8. A B C
9. A B C
10. A B C

Integrated Spelling

Unit 4: Writing Activities

WORDS TO WATCH FOR

uncle
usually
suppose
thank you
minute
mom's
no one
nowhere

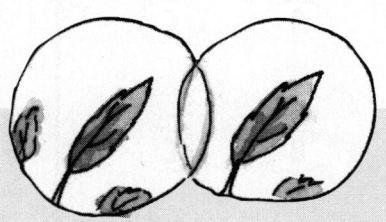

Nature Watch

Work as a group to watch some insects or animals in your neighborhood. You might choose a bat, songbird, butterfly, lizard, or other animal. Describe its color. Try to watch for the times of day when the animal eats, sleeps, and moves around. Look for other animals of the same type that live nearby. As a group, write a paragraph about the animal you have watched. Check your Spelling Log as you write. Display the completed paragraph on the bulletin board to share with others.

Tips for Spelling Success

- Your paragraph will be easy to read if you are careful to spell words correctly.
- Keep your handwriting neat.
- Make correct spelling changes before adding *-ed* or *-ing*.
- Some Words to Watch For are at the left.

Where to Learn More About Nature

What do you like best about nature study? List your interests and any questions you have. Show your list to a librarian, who can help you find books about a particular subject. Keep a record of the titles of the books you read. For example, your list might include books about pond animals, books about birds of prey, and books that describe how herders raise sheep in dry territory.

Tips for Spelling Success

- Do some of the words in your list look wrong?
- When you take notes, make sure to write clearly.
- Then, if you are asked to write a book report, it will be easy to spell all the words correctly.
- Check a dictionary if you're still not sure of the spelling.

Name _____

Nature Diary

What kinds of plants and animals live near you? Are the animals desert reptiles, such as lizards and snakes? Are they pond creatures, such as goldfish and dragonflies? Do the trees stay green all year? Spend fifteen minutes writing in a notebook or diary, describing what you can see from your home or from a park nearby. Describe the sky, land, water, plants, and animals. Look in your Spelling Log for vivid words to help you write more exactly. You may want to continue writing in your notebook or diary each day.

Tips for Spelling Success

- To make your writing understandable, you'll need to spell each word correctly.
- After you proofread for ideas, read each entry backward one word at a time.
- Sound out each word, listen carefully, and look for errors in spelling the sounds.
- Double-check words that show possession, such as *boys'* and *father's*, and contractions, such as *we've* and *I'd*.

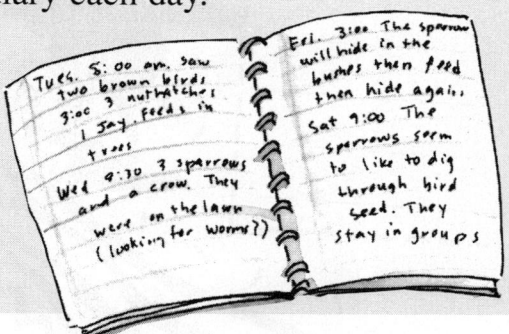

Change-a-Letter

Add and subtract letters from the words below to write Spelling Words.

be + slide – l + s = _____

alone + g – e = _____

w + hat + 's = _____

talking – l = _____

Tips for Spelling Success

- To improve your spelling, find words you have misspelled more than once.
- In your Spelling Log, make a list of these hard-to-spell words.

Integrated Spelling LESSON 24 • REVIEW

SPELLING WORDS

1. cherries
2. fried
3. flies
4. puppies
5. ladies
6. carried
7. dried
8. cries
9. studied
10. tries
11. married
12. buried

Look for other words in which *y* is changed to *i* before adding an ending. Add the words to the lists. You might find *cities* in the telephone book. Where might you find *spied*?

13. _____
14. _____
15. _____

Changing *y* to *i*

Each Spelling Word has an ending that was added after *y* was changed to *i*.

Sort the Spelling Words in a way that will help you remember them. Two example words have been given.

▶ When a word ends in a consonant and *y*, change *y* to *i* before adding *-es* or *-ed*.

Name _____

Strategy Workshop

SPELLING CLUES: Spelling Rules When you proofread, remember the "change *y* to *i*" rule. If a word ends in a consonant and *y*, change *y* to *i* before adding *-es* or *-ed*.

Add the ending and write a Spelling Word.

1. cherry + es
2. study + ed
3. lady + es
4. puppy + es
5. carry + ed
6. marry + ed
7. dry + ed

Proofread the tongue twisters. Circle the spelling errors, and write the correct spellings.

8. Fred's fifteen fryed fish fed five friends.
9. Do fleis fly from far to near?
10. "Come, Cliff," cryes Caitlyn, "and count the clouds."
11. Bridget's bulldog buryed big bones beside Bob's box.
12. Tiffany Tuttle took ten tryes to tell her tale.

1. _____
2. _____
3. _____
4. _____
5. _____
6. _____
7. _____

8. _____
9. _____
10. _____
11. _____
12. _____

Integrated Spelling

School WORDS

- students
- taught
- recess
- lessons

SPELLING LOG Think about how you might use these words in your writing, and add them to your Spelling Log.

1. _____
2. _____
3. _____
4. _____

5. _____
6. _____
7. _____

8. _____
9. _____
10. _____

Name _____

Vocabulary WordShop

Write the School Words to finish the time line below.

1. 8:00 A.M. The ____ arrived before ten each morning.
2. 8:30 A.M. Within a half hour, ____ began again.
3. 10:00 A.M. The first classes ended then with ____.
4. 10:30 A.M. Mrs. Calley ____ them arithmetic.

WHAT'S IN A WORD?

A *thesaurus* is a book for word detectives! A thesaurus lists collections of words that have similar meanings. You can use a thesaurus to add variety to your writing or speaking. For example, under *teach* you might find *instruct* or *educate*.

5–7. List three other words that might appear in a thesaurus under the entry *teach*.

8–10. Maybe you have what it takes to be a teacher. List three things you know how to do well enough to teach someone else.

Name _____

SOUND-ALIKES Rhymes link words into patterns that help you spell. Sometimes the last word in a line of a poem rhymes with a word at the end of another line. Write rhyming words to finish the poem. Use the underlined word in each pair of lines as a hint.

The pupils ran across the <u>grass</u>
   To be on time for their first __1__ .
"Use your textbooks, slates, and <u>chalk</u>.
   Stop the chatter! Stop the __2__ !"
Mr. Adams points and <u>asks</u>,
   "Who can do these spelling __3__ ?"
"We'll do them all," the students <u>say</u>,
   "If at recess we can __4__ !"

NAME GAME Many people have unusual names, and for many different reasons.

5–8. Tell how you got your name. Then list three unusual names you have heard, and guess how their owners got their names.

FUN WITH A PARTNER You and a partner can write Spelling Words on the board leaving out some of the letters. Then trade places and complete each other's words. See how many of the Spelling Words each of you can complete.

1. _____
2. _____
3. _____
4. _____

5. _____
   _____
   _____
6. _____
   _____
7. _____
   _____
8. _____
   _____

Integrated Spelling

SPELLING WORDS

1. cotton
2. better
3. hello
4. follow
5. funny
6. dinner
7. supper
8. bottom
9. village
10. written
11. yellow
12. scatter

Look for other two-syllable words like *dinner* to add to the lists. On a menu, you may find *platter* or *batter*. On a billboard, you may find *kitten* or *dollars*.

13. _____
14. _____
15. _____

Words Like *dinner*

Each Spelling Word has two syllables. Look for the doubled consonant in the middle of each word as in *dinner*.

Sort the Spelling Words in a way that will help you remember them. Four example words have been given.

▶ Some two-syllable words have doubled consonants in the middle. Words like this are usually divided into two syllables between these two consonants.

110   LESSON 26   Integrated Spelling

Name _____

Strategy Workshop

SPELLING CLUES: Smaller Words

Look for the small words that may be in larger words. Write the Spelling Words that have these smaller words.

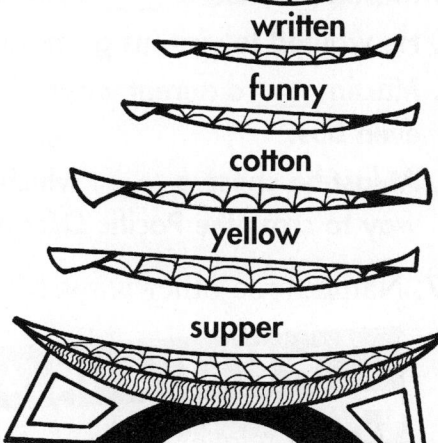

- scatter
- written
- funny
- cotton
- yellow
- supper

1. ends with *ton*
2. begins with *yell*
3. begins with *sup*
4. ends with *ten*
5. begins with *fun*
6. begins with *scat*

1. _____
2. _____
3. _____
4. _____
5. _____
6. _____

Write the Spelling Words that fit these clues.

7. rhymes with *sweater*
8. is a meal that rhymes with *thinner*
9. names a cluster of houses
10. is a greeting

7. _____
8. _____
9. _____
10. _____

FUN WITH WORDS Some clues can show you what a word is by telling you what it's not. Write a Spelling Word for each clue.

11. don't lead
12. not the top

11. _____
12. _____

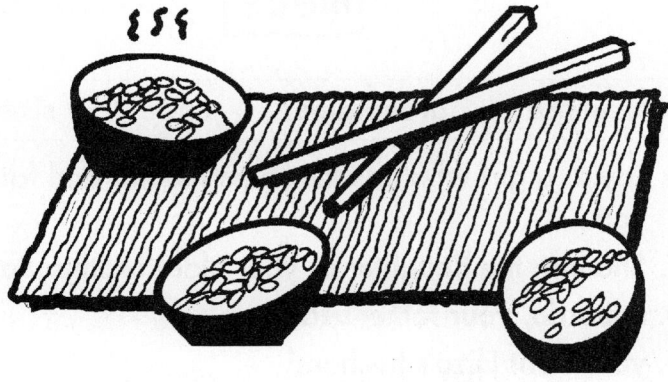

Integrated Spelling LESSON 26

Traveling WORDS

journey
explored
homeland
steamship

SPELLING LOG Imagine a cartoon about a character who never stops traveling. Use the Traveling Words to tell a short story about the character. Then add the words to your Spelling Log.

1. _____
2. _____
3. _____
4. _____

5. _____
6. _____
7. _____

8. _____
9. _____
10. _____
11. _____

Vocabulary WordShop

TRAVELING WORDS Help Martin the Mouse plan a journey from the United States to Japan. Write a Traveling Word to complete each part of his travel plans.

1. Martin planned a ____ from his home in California.
2. He wanted to visit his grandfather's ____.
3. Martin ____ different ways of travel — boats, planes, even bus.
4. At last he chose a ____, which he thought was the safest way to cross the Pacific Ocean.

5–7. Name three other ways Martin might travel.

WHAT'S IN A WORD?

Family relationships can be confusing. The word *family* comes from the Latin word *familia*, which means "household." Imagine you are in this family. Match the words in the box to the descriptions of the members of your imaginary family. Then write the words.

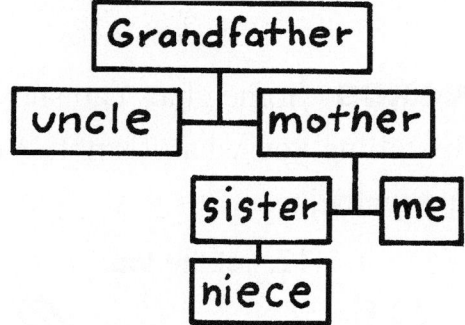

niece   grandfather   uncle   sister

8. Layla, a girl who has the same mother and father as you
9. Shanna, the daughter of your older brother Sam
10. Eduardo, your father's father
11. your Aunt Eliza's husband

Name _____

FAMILY WORDS A dictionary of foreign words can tell you how to say family words in another language.

In French, your Aunt Mary is *Tante Marie.*
In Spanish, your Uncle Peter is *Tío Pedro.*
In Italian, your Grandfather Anthony is *Nono Antonio.*

What would you call these relatives in English?
1. (Spanish) Tía Angelina
2. (French) Grandmère Marthe
3. (French) Oncle Claude
4. (Italian) Nono Paolo

1. _____
   _____
2. _____
   _____
   _____
3. _____
   _____
4. _____
   _____

RELATIVE WORDS Think about all the people to whom you are related. Write your name in the center of a web on another sheet of paper. Then write the names of your family members all around your name. Write a family word below each name.

JUST FOR FUN Make flash cards. On each card, write a word that rhymes with one of the Spelling Words. For example, write *letter* as the rhyme for *better*. Hold up each card, and ask a partner to spell the Spelling Word that rhymes with your word. Then have your partner write the rhyming Spelling Word on the back of the card.

Integrated Spelling   LESSON 26

Name ______________________

SPELLING WORDS

1. player
2. farmer
3. lonely
4. playful
5. owner
6. really
7. leader
8. careful
9. slowly
10. useful
11. thankful
12. quickly

Your Own WORDS

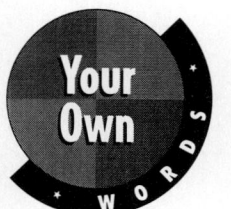

Look for other words with suffixes to add to the lists. You may find *singer* or *specially* in a television program guide. A sports magazine may contain *harmful* or *scoreless.*

13. ______________________

14. ______________________

15. ______________________

Words with Suffixes

Each Spelling Word ends with a suffix. Look at the letters that form each ending.

Sort the Spelling Words in a way that will help you remember them. Three example words have been given.

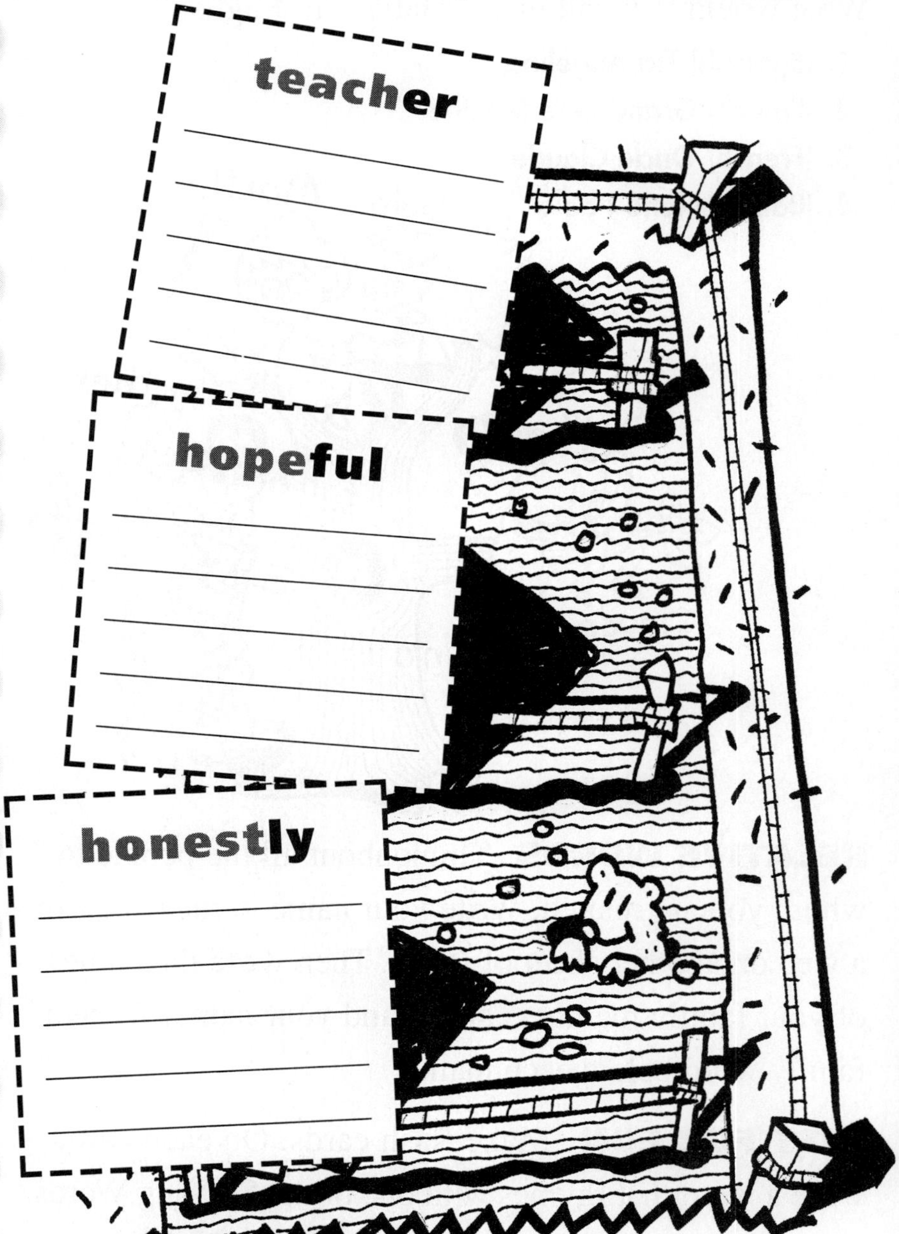

teacher
hopeful
honestly

▶ **You can add suffixes to some words without making any spelling changes in the base word.**

Name _____

Strategy Workshop

PROOFREADING: Word Parts When a word has a suffix, break the word into two parts. Think about how the word is spelled without its suffix. Then add the suffix.

Add a suffix from the box to write a Spelling Word.

```
-er          -ful          -ly
```

1. real   2. thank   3. use
4. farm   5. lone   6. slow

HAPPY ENDINGS Correct these three mini-stories by circling words that need suffixes. Then add suffixes to the circled words to form Spelling Words.

7–8. Taylor wants to be first in line. She will be the lead. She says, "Be care when you cross the street."

9–10. Who is the own of this kitten? It is black with white paws. It is very play.

11–12. Jamal is the best play on our team. He hits the ball well and runs the bases quick.

1. _____
2. _____
3. _____
4. _____
5. _____
6. _____

7. _____
8. _____
9. _____
10. _____
11. _____
12. _____

Integrated Spelling

Flower WORDS

pod
petals
bloom
blossom

SPELLING LOG Think about how you might use these words in your writing, and add them to your Spelling Log.

1. _____
2. _____
3. _____
4. _____

Vocabulary WordShop

Use the Flower Words to finish the story below.

Jesse was planting a garden. He made holes in the dirt. Jesse opened the __1__ and took out the seeds. He planted a seed in each hole. Soon there was a __2__ on one plant. Jesse tried to count the yellow __3__, but they were tightly closed. He closed his eyes and made a wish. When he was done, one __4__ had opened.

5-8. Think about a garden you might like to plant. Tell what types of flowers and plants would be there. Write your list on the lines.

5. _____
6. _____
7. _____
8. _____

Name _____

WHAT'S IN A WORD?

The word *flora* means "the plant life of a region." The word comes from the name of the Roman goddess of flowers, Flora. Do any of your friends have first names that are also the names of flowers? Solve each puzzle below with the name of a flower that is also a girl's name.

R + 🌹 – n = **1**

I + risk – k = **2**

Vio + ✉ – ter = **3**

🦁 – on + ly = **4**

COMPOUND WORDS Did you know that the names of some flowers are compound words? A compound word is made by joining two or more smaller words. Solve each puzzle below. Write the compound word that is also the name of a flower.

snap + 🐉 = **5**

☀ + 🌻 = **6**

blue + 🔔 = **7**

WITH A PARTNER Divide the list of Spelling Words into two lists of six words each. Take one list and have your partner take the other. Circle the suffixes of all your words. Then say to your partner the first word on your list, *without* its suffix. Have your partner spell the whole word, including the suffix. If your partner misspells the word, spell it correctly. Take turns until you have used all the words.

1. _____
2. _____
3. _____
4. _____

5. _____
6. _____
7. _____

Integrated Spelling   LESSON 27

SPELLING WORDS

1. happy
2. any
3. very
4. pretty
5. cookie
6. money
7. movie
8. turkey
9. every
10. party
11. sorry
12. heavy

Look for other words that end with the same sound as *happy* to add to the lists. You might find *penny* on a sign at the bank or *family* on the ticket window of a movie theater.

13. _____
14. _____
15. _____

Name _____

Words That End Like *happy*

Each Spelling Word ends with the same sound you hear at the end of *happy*. Look at the letter or letters that spell that ending sound.

Sort the Spelling Words in a way that will help you remember them. Two example words have been given. Fill in the other one as you are sorting.

silly

brownie

▶ The ending sound you hear in *happy* can be spelled *y*, *ie*, or *ey*.

118 LESSON 28   Integrated Spelling

Name _____

Strategy Workshop

PROOFREADING: Using a Dictionary When you proofread, circle words that may contain errors. Use a dictionary to check the spelling.

1–4. Which words below do not look right to you? Circle any words that you think are misspelled. Check the correct spelling in a dictionary, and write the word.

1. any   hevy   pretty
2. cooky   money   sorry
3. every   movie   turky
4. happy   party   verey

1. _____
2. _____
3. _____
4. _____

5–11. Proofread the notice. Circle the misspelled words, and write the correct spellings.

NOTICE: The First Street Movy Theater is closed for the week. We are sorrey for the delay. Aney questions may be telephoned to the manager. First Street will reopen on Friday with a pizza partie. We know you will like our prettie new wallpaper. Come and register for the monie: $50 first place, $25 second place, and five third places of $5 each. Evry customer has a chance to win!

5. _____
6. _____
7. _____
8. _____
9. _____
10. _____
11. _____

TRY THIS! Write a Spelling Word to complete this alphabetized list of words.

happen   happening   happily   <u> 12 </u>   heavy

12. _____

Integrated Spelling   **LESSON 28   119**

School Supply WORDS

crayon
knapsack
locker
worksheet

SPELLING LOG Think about how you might use these words in your writing, and add them to your Spelling Log.

1. _____
2. _____
3. _____

Name _____

Vocabulary WordShop

Write the School Supply Word that has each of these word histories.

1. The word _____ comes from the German word *knappen* added to the Dutch word *zak*, meaning "bag."
2. The word _____ comes from the French word *craie*.
3. The word _____ comes from the Old English word *loc*.

COMPOUND WORDS Compound words are made of two or more smaller words that are often written together. Here are two examples:

work +  = workhorse

work +  = worktable

Solve the word-and-picture puzzle with a compound word that is also a School Supply Word.

work +  = <u>4</u>

5–7. All the compound words above contain the word *work* as one of their smaller words. Write some compound words that contain the word *school* as one of their smaller words. Write them on the lines.

4. _____
5. _____
6. _____
7. _____

120   LESSON 28

Integrated Spelling

Name _____

WHAT'S IN A WORD?

Words are like countries—they each have a history. The word *gum* comes from the Old English word *goma*, which means "roof of the mouth." Chewing gum has been around for hundreds of years. It was a favorite of Native American children long before Columbus sailed to the New World.

1. Name two other things or activities that Native Americans enjoyed long before Columbus sailed to the New World.

2–13. Work with a partner. Write each Spelling Word on a separate index card or on a small piece of paper. Arrange the cards or papers in alphabetical order. Then write the words alphabetically on the lines.

JUST FOR FUN Study the list of Spelling Words for one minute. Then, without looking back at the list, see how many of the Spelling Words you can write correctly. Have a partner check and give hints for any words you may have left out.

1. _____
   _____
   _____

2. _____
3. _____
4. _____
5. _____
6. _____
7. _____
8. _____
9. _____
10. _____
11. _____
12. _____
13. _____

Integrated Spelling　　　**LESSON 28**

Name _____

Compound Words

SPELLING WORDS

1. outside
2. bedroom
3. football
4. airplane
5. someone
6. birthday
7. cannot
8. classroom
9. homework
10. playground
11. everything
12. sidewalk

Look for other compound words to add to the lists. You might find *mainland* or *shoreline* in a geography book. In a science article, you might find *backbone* or *eardrum*.

13. _____
14. _____
15. _____

Each Spelling Word is a compound word. Look at the word parts.

Sort the Spelling Words in a way that will help you remember them.

compound words that name places
_____
_____
_____
_____
_____

compound words that name things
_____
_____
_____
_____
_____

other compound words
_____
_____
_____

▶ A compound word is a word formed by joining two smaller words.

122 LESSON 29

Integrated Spelling

Name _____

Strategy Workshop

SPELLING CLUES: Smaller Words Think about the spelling of the smaller words that make up a compound word. That will make it easier to spell the compound word.

Write the Spelling Word that contains the smaller word.

1. walk
2. day
3. bed
4. foot
5. work
6. play

7–11. Complete the diary entry. Use the smaller word in parentheses as a clue, and then write the Spelling Word.

> February 3
>
> Dear Diary,
>   I (**7. not**) tell you how happy I am! At school, I thought (**8. some**) in the (**9. class**) would make fun of my name. But instead, (**10. thing**) turned out fine. And when we went (**11. side**) to play, I made many friends!

1. _____
2. _____
3. _____
4. _____
5. _____
6. _____

7. _____
8. _____
9. _____
10. _____
11. _____

FUN WITH WORDS Write a Spelling Word to complete the joke.

Why didn't the boy get the joke about the __12__ ? It went over his head!

12. _____

Integrated Spelling

LESSON 29   123

Name _____

Championship WORDS

hero
special
proud
title

SPELLING LOG Think about how you might use these words in your writing, and add them to your Spelling Log.

1. _____
2. _____
3. _____
4. _____

Vocabulary WordShop

Use the Championship Words to complete the newspaper headlines.

Extra, extra! Read all about it!

STUDENT WINS _1_ OF BEST SPELLER IN STATE!

"CHAMPION SPELLER IS A _2_!" SAYS SCHOOL PRINCIPAL

"WE ARE SO _3_ OF OUR CHILD!" PARENTS SHOUT

BEST SPELLER RECEIVES BOOKS AS _4_ PRIZE!

5. Write one more headline about a champion speller.

5. _____
_____
_____
_____

6–8. Then add your own words about championships on the lines.

6. _____
7. _____
8. _____

124 LESSON 29

Integrated Spelling

Name _____

WHAT'S IN A WORD?

The word *title* has several different meanings. In "When Jo Louis Won the Title," *title* refers to the championship that the boxer Joe Louis won. But in the story, *title* also refers to Jo's name, because the story tells why she was named Jo.

Explain the meaning of *title* in each sentence.
1. What is the <u>title</u> of the book you're reading?
2. After finishing Medical School, Judy earned the <u>title</u> of Doctor.

MULTIPLE MEANINGS Some words have more than one meaning. Write one word that makes sense in both blanks in the pair of sentences. Use the pictures as clues.

3. Do you write with a pencil or with a ____?
The pigs were kept in a ____.

4. Dan wears ____ to see better.
Pour the juice into these two ____.

5. A ____ flew out of the cave.
She swung the ____ to hit the baseball.

6. A ____ equals twelve inches.
The big toe on my left ____ hurts.

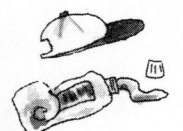
7. This ____ is too small for my head.
Put the ____ back on the toothpaste tube.

MIX AND MATCH Work with a partner. Each partner writes six Spelling Words in large letters on index cards. Then cut apart each compound word to make two words. Mix up the cards, and take turns. See how many of the Spelling Words each of you can put together again.

1. _____
2. _____
   _____
   _____
   _____
3. _____
4. _____
5. _____
6. _____
7. _____

Integrated Spelling   LESSON 29   125

SPELLING WORDS

1. rainy
2. muddy
3. sandy
4. windy
5. shiny
6. furry
7. sleepy
8. icy
9. nosy
10. salty
11. sticky
12. foggy

Look for other words that end in *-y* to add to the lists. You might find *cloudy* and *muggy* in a weather report. You might see *spicy* and *tasty* on a menu.

13. _____
14. _____
15. _____

Suffix: -y

Each Spelling Word has the suffix *-y*. Look for changes in the spelling of the base word when this ending is added.

Sort the Spelling Words in a way that will help you remember them. Three example words have been given.

▶ If a word ends in two consonants or in vowel-vowel-consonant, just add *-y*.

▶ If a word ends in a vowel and consonant, double the consonant and add *-y*.

▶ If a word ends in a consonant and *e*, drop the *e* and add *-y*.

126 LESSON 30

Integrated Spelling

Strategy Workshop

PROOFREADING: Word Parts When you proofread, pay attention to words endings. Be sure that you make any spelling changes that are needed before adding -*y*.

Add the -*y* ending and write a Spelling Word.
1. nose + y
2. stick + y
3. fur + y
4. shine + y
5. salt + y
6. sleep + y

7–12. Proofread the diary entries. Be sure to check the spelling of words ending in -*y*. Circle the spelling errors, and write the words correctly.

December 8—We arrived in our new town. It's so rainey. I know the ground will be mudy tomorrow.

December 9—Today the rain stopped, but now it's windey. I walked along the sandey beach and got sand in my eyes.

December 10—I can't believe how fogy the mornings are here. When it turns icey, I hope I can go ice-skating!

1. _____
2. _____
3. _____
4. _____
5. _____
6. _____

7. _____
8. _____
9. _____
10. _____
11. _____
12. _____

Integrated Spelling

Name _____

Immigration
WORDS

immigrant
migration
settler
trek

SPELLING LOG Think about how you might use these words in your writing, and add them to your Spelling Log.

1. _____
2. _____
3. _____
4. _____

5. _____
   _____
   _____
   _____
   _____
   _____

6. _____
7. _____
8. _____

Vocabulary WordShop

How has immigration changed over the years? To find out, complete the chart by using Immigration Words.

IMMIGRATION	
Long Ago	**Today**
People would __1__ across the land by wagon or on foot.	People travel by car, bus, train, or airplane.
A __2__ would often build a home on land that no one lived on.	A person settles where others already live.
An __3__ almost never got to visit his or her homeland after moving.	A person has a better chance of visiting his or her homeland again.
The average __4__ was no more than a few hundred miles.	People today move as much as thousands of miles.

5. Write other sentences that tell about immigration today or long ago.

6–8. Then write words about immigration on the lines at the left.

128 LESSON 30   Integrated Spelling

Name _____

WHAT'S IN A WORD?

When you come to a new place to live, you are an *immigrant*. But first you must be an *emigrant*—one who leaves the old place. An emigrant leaves, and an immigrant arrives. The words *emigrant* and *immigrant* are *antonyms*—words that are opposites.

1. What differences do you find in the spellings of *immigrant* and *emigrant*?

ANTONYMS Choose a word from the box that is an antonym for the underlined word. Write the word you chose.

| shut | exit | close | before | found |

2. When you wake up, you <u>open</u> your eyes. When you go to sleep, you _____ them.
3. When you go into a room, you <u>enter</u> it. When you go out of a room, you _____ it.
4. You do the second problem <u>after</u> the first one. You do the first problem _____ the second one.
5. When you go into a room, you <u>open</u> the door. When you leave a room, you _____ it.
6. When you don't know where something is, you've <u>lost</u> it. When you do know where something lost is, you've _____ it.

STORY TIME Write each Spelling Word on a separate index card. Mix the cards and pick one. Start a silly story that uses that word in a sentence. Then have a partner pick another card and use the word in a sentence to continue the story. Try to keep the story going until you have used as many of the Spelling Words as possible.

1. _____
_____
_____
_____
_____
_____
_____
_____
2. _____
3. _____
4. _____
5. _____
6. _____

Integrated Spelling

Name _____

Practice Test

A. Read each sentence. Find the correctly spelled word to complete each sentence. On the answer sheet, mark the letter that is next to that word.

Example: The ____ sailed.
   A bote   B boat   C boht

1. Many ____ got on the boat.
   A ladys   B ladeys   C ladies

2. They ____ large bags.
   A carried   B carryed   C carreyed

3. The boat sailed from the ____.
   A vilage   B village   C villige

4. Sea birds began to ____.
   A scater   B scatter   C scattar

5. The people were served ____.
   A suppar   B supar   C supper

6. The boat ____ made its way on the sea.
   A slowly   B sloly   C slowley

7. Everyone was ____ for the trip.
   A thankfel   B thankful   C thankfull

8. The ____ of the group spoke.
   A leader   B leeder   C leadar

9. She said that ____ person was lucky.
   A everie   B everey   C every

10. They would be ____ in their new home.
   A happey   B happy   C happie

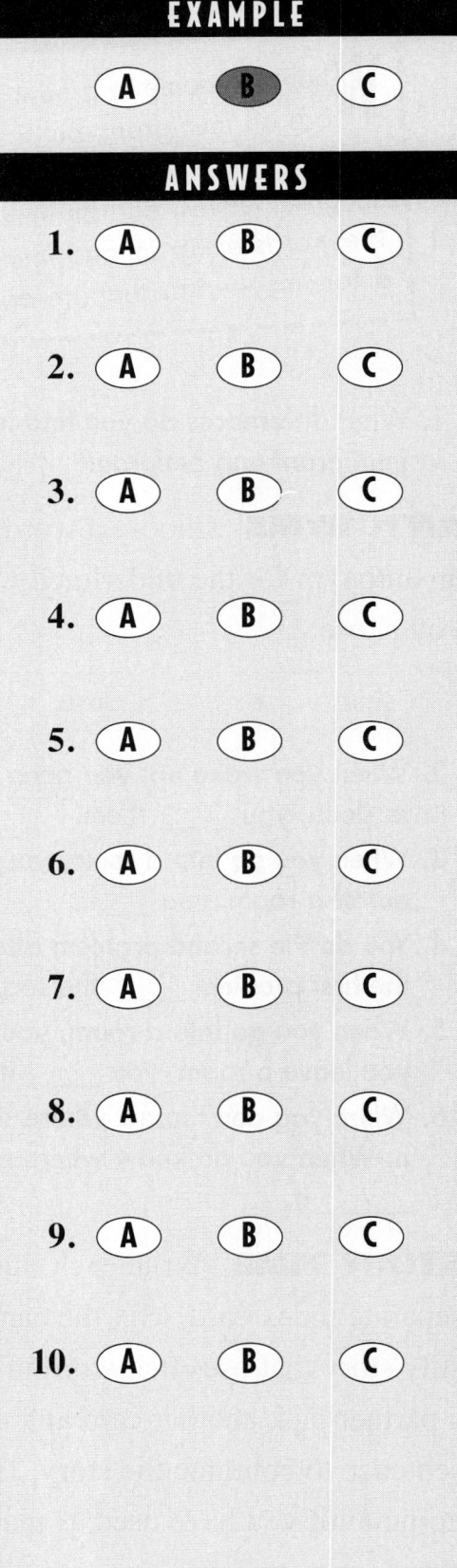

Name _____

B. Read each sentence. Find the correctly spelled word to complete each sentence. On the answer sheet, mark the letter that is next to that word.

1. The people looked ____.
   A out-side   B outside   C out side

2. They took ____ they had brought.
   A every thing   B every-thing   C everything

3. Soon ____ led them off the boat.
   A someone   B some one   C some-one

4. The coin was very ____.
   A shiney   B shinie   C shiny

5. The ____ people looked around.
   A sleepy   B sleepey   C sleepie

6. They walked on the ____ ground.
   A muddie   B muddey   C muddy

7. The bags were very ____.
   A heavie   B heavy   C heavey

8. No one felt ____.
   A sorry   B sorrie   C sorey

9. They were ____ glad they were safe.
   A verie   B very   C verey

10. No one was ____ in the new land.
    A lonly   B lonelly   C lonely

ANSWERS

1. A B C
2. A B C
3. A B C
4. A B C
5. A B C
6. A B C
7. A B C
8. A B C
9. A B C
10. A B C

Integrated Spelling   LESSON 31 • REVIEW

Name _____

Unit 5: Writing Activities

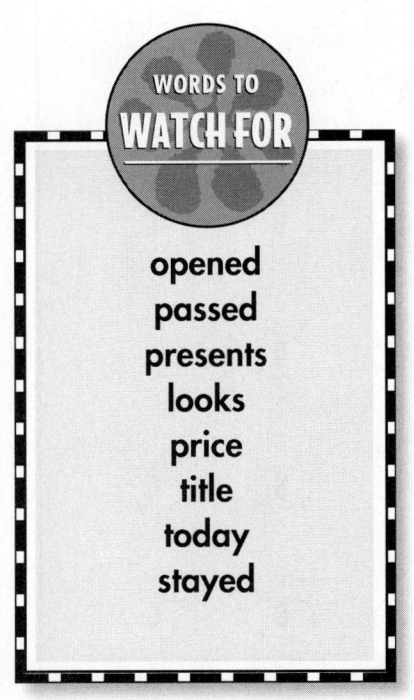

WORDS TO WATCH FOR

opened
passed
presents
looks
price
title
today
stayed

Book Chat

Do you ever pretend that you're one of the characters in the book you're reading? You would be able to live in their house and go to the same places the characters in the book go. Pick a book that you are reading, or a favorite book that you have read before. Decide which character you would like to be. Write a dialogue that tells what you, as the character, would say to someone to get that person interested in your book.

Tips for Spelling Success

- Be sure to place quotation marks around the exact words that you and the other person speak.
- On the left are some words you might use in your dialogue. Watch out for the tricky spelling of some of these words.

What a Trip!

Have you traveled somewhere interesting? Maybe you and your family went on a vacation. Maybe you read an interesting book about a faraway place. Or maybe you discovered an interesting place right in your neighborhood. Write a personal narrative that tells about these travels or adventures. Tell where you or the people in the book went, and what you or they did. Draw a map that shows this place.

Tips for Spelling Success

- Use time-order words to tell about the things you did. Describe what you did first, next, later, and last.
- Check to make sure that you've spelled all singular and plural possessive nouns correctly.

Name _____

Reading Greeting

Think of a good book you've read. How about telling a friend about it? Design a greeting card that shows what the book is about. On the front and back of the card, draw pictures of the people and places in the book. On the inside of the card, describe the book. (But don't give away the ending!) When your card is finished, present it to a friend.

Tips for Spelling Success
- Make sure that all names of specific people and places begin with a capital letter.
- Make sure you write the author's name correctly, too.

Get the Picture?

Here's a game to play with a partner. Choose a Spelling Word. Draw a picture that shows part of the word. Then write letters to complete the word. For example:

tur +  = turkey

writ + 🔟 = written

☀ + day = Sunday

Now choose your own words to draw. See whether your partner can guess your Spelling Word.

Tips for Spelling Success
- For each word you choose, say each part of the word carefully. Think about how to spell each part of the word.

Integrated Spelling

Name _____

Words That End Like *never*

Each Spelling Word ends with the sound you hear at the end of *never*. Look at the letters that spell that ending sound.

Sort the Spelling Words in a way that will help you remember them. Three example words have been given.

SPELLING WORDS

1. river
2. water
3. ever
4. number
5. sugar
6. dollar
7. color
8. favor
9. author
10. never
11. together
12. mirror

Look for other words with the same sound you hear at the end of *never* to add to the lists. You may find *calendar* in your math book, *equator* in your social studies book, and *flower* in your science book.

13. _____
14. _____
15. _____

▶ The ending sound you hear in *never* can be spelled *er*, *ar*, or *or*.

134   LESSON 32   Integrated Spelling

Name _____

Strategy Workshop

PROOFREADING: Classifying Errors When you proofread, keep track of your spelling errors. See what kinds of mistakes you usually make and then work to avoid them.

What's wrong with each word? Follow the directions to write the correct spelling.

> watar   suger   togethar   rivor   faver

1–3. For three words, change the spelling of the ending sound to *er*.

4. For one word, change the spelling of the ending sound to *ar*.

5. For one word, change the spelling of the ending sound to *or*.

6–11. Proofread the advertisement below. Circle the six spelling errors, and then write the words correctly.

> Buy the numbar-one best-selling book *I Need My Space . . . in Outer Space!*
>
> It's the best thing that auther Carol Manten has evor written!
>
> Once you start reading, you'll nevar want to stop!
>
> Buy the book this week and save one doller!
>
> Included are great photos in exciting coler!

FUN WITH WORDS Write a Spelling Word to complete the riddle.

Where can you find someone who looks just like you?

Where?

In the __12__!

1. _____
2. _____
3. _____
4. _____
5. _____

6. _____
7. _____
8. _____
9. _____
10. _____
11. _____

12. _____

Integrated Spelling

Planet
* WORDS *

axis
atmosphere
ellipse
gravity

SPELLING LOG Think about how you might use these words in your writing, and add them to your Spelling Log.

1. _____
2. _____
3. _____
4. _____

5. _____
6. _____
7. _____
8. _____

Vocabulary WordShop

Use the Planet Words to help the robot answer the questions.

1. **Question:** Why can't people live on the moon?
   Answer: Because the moon has no __1__, or air. People need air to live.

2. **Question:** Do people weigh the same on the moon as on Earth?
   Answer: No, because __2__ on the moon is weaker than on Earth. If you weighed 60 pounds on Earth, you'd weigh only 10 pounds on the moon.

3. **Question:** Does the moon move?
   Answer: Yes. It spins on its __3__, an imaginary line through its north and south poles. It also travels around the Earth.

4. **Question:** Does the moon travel in a straight line?
   Answer: No. It travels along a curved path, called an __4__.

5–8. Write other planet words you know on the lines at the left.

Name _____

WHAT'S IN A WORD?

The word *atmosphere* comes from the Greek word *atmos* and the Latin word *sphaera*. *Atmos* means "vapor," which is a kind of gas that exists in the air. *Sphaera* means "sphere," which is a round body. The word part *sphere* is found in many other words.

1. Write at least one more word you know that ends in *sphere*.

WORDS FROM GREEK Use the words from the box to answer the questions. The information below gives important clues.

| phases | telescope | asteroid | cycle |

2. This word names a long tube that helps you see things that are far away. It starts the same way as the word *telephone*. What is the word?

3. This word names a cycle of changes such as those the moon makes each month. What is the word?

4. This word refers to a circle. If you add the word part *bi-* or *tri-* to it, you have something you can ride around the block. What is the word?

5. This word describes one of the small planetoids mostly found between Mars and Jupiter. It contains the word part *aster*, meaning "star." What is the word?

MIRROR IMAGE The following message is written in code. Try to read it. If you need help, use a mirror. Then try to write some of the Spelling Words in mirror writing.

Have fun reading this.

1. _____
   _____
   _____

2. _____
3. _____
4. _____
5. _____

Integrated Spelling

Words That End Like *little*

SPELLING WORDS

1. little
2. apple
3. table
4. middle
5. normal
6. able
7. final
8. bubble
9. castle
10. purple
11. total
12. handle

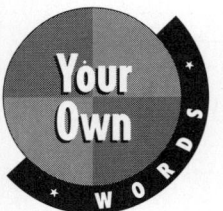

Look for other words with the same sound you hear at the end of *little* to add to the lists. You'll probably find *circle* or *numeral* in your math book. You might find *mineral* in your science book and *capital* in your social studies book.

13. _____
14. _____
15. _____

Each Spelling Word ends with the sound you hear at the end of *little*. Look at the letters that spell that ending sound.

Sort the Spelling Words in a way that will help you remember them. One example word is given. Fill in the other one as you are sorting.

▶ The ending sound you hear in *little* can be spelled *le* or *al*.

138   LESSON 33   Integrated Spelling

Name _____

Strategy Workshop

PROOFREADING: Working Together When you proofread, work with a partner. Read the words aloud as your partner looks at the spelling. Then switch roles.

1–5. Work with a partner to circle the five words that are misspelled. Then write the correct spelling for each one.

bubbel	handle	normel	little
able	castal	purpel	apple
final	totle	table	middle

1. _____
2. _____
3. _____
4. _____
5. _____

6–11. Work with a partner to proofread the following joke. Circle the six spelling errors, and then write the words correctly.

Banker: Are you abel to handal money well? Would you like to turn a littal into a lot?
Customer: You bet!
Banker: Good. I'll show you how to double your money. First take out a dollar bill. Now put it on the middel of this tabal.
Customer: Okay. Now what?
Banker: For the finel step, just fold the bill in half. Now you've doubled it!

6. _____
7. _____
8. _____
9. _____
10. _____
11. _____

FUN WITH WORDS Write a Spelling Word to complete the cartoon.

What's the difference between an __12__ and money?
What?
Money doesn't grow on trees!

12. _____

Integrated Spelling

Money WORDS

million
hundred
thousand
interest

SPELLING LOG Think about how you might use these words in your writing, and add them to your Spelling Log.

1. _____
2. _____
3. _____
4. _____

5. _____
   _____
   _____

6. _____
7. _____
8. _____

Name _____

Vocabulary WordShop

Use the Money Words to complete the problem below.

Suppose you took a job for thirty days. At the start your boss said, "You have a choice. You can receive $1,000 for the entire job. Or you can be paid one penny for the first day, and I'll double your pay each day after that." Would you take the **1** dollars? If you take the second offer instead, you're smart! Here's why:

On the fourteenth day, you would receive $81.92. On the fifteenth day, you'd get double that, which is more than a **2** dollars! Believe it or not, by the twenty-seventh day, you'd receive more than $600,000! On the twenty-eighth day, you'd get double that, which is more than a **3** dollars! Even a bank doesn't pay that much **4**!

5. Make up your own money problem using numbers.
6–8. Write your money words on the lines at the left.

Name _____

WHAT'S IN A WORD?

The word *million* comes from the Latin word *mille*, meaning "thousand." A million is equal to a thousand thousands.

```
    1,000    one thousand
  x 1,000    one thousand
1,000,000    one million
```

1. Write the word that means "one thousand millions."

MILL- WORDS Many words start with the word part *mill-*. Their meanings have to do with either "a thousand" or "a million." Use the words from the box to complete the sentences below. If you like, use a dictionary for help.

> millionaire   millimeter   milligram   millennium   millipede

2. It equals one thousandth of a gram. The weight is called a _____.

3. It's the name of someone who owns at least a million dollars. The word is _____.

4. It's the name of a creature that has so many legs, there seem to be a thousand! The creature is called a _____.

5. It's the name for a period of one thousand years. The year 2000 marks the end of the second _____.

6. It equals one thousandth of a meter. The measurement is called a _____.

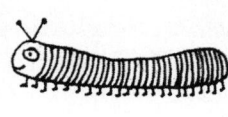  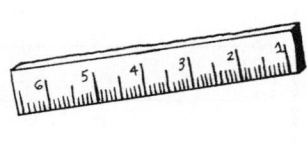

RIDDLE TIME Choose six Spelling Words. Write a riddle for each word. (The words may appear in the question or the answer.) Challenge classmates to answer each riddle and to correctly spell each Spelling Word.

1. _____
2. _____
3. _____
4. _____
5. _____
6. _____

Integrated Spelling   **LESSON 33**

Name _____

Words That End Like *seven*

Each Spelling Word ends with the sound you hear at the end of *seven*. Look at the letters that spell that ending sound.

Sort the Spelling Words in a way that will help you remember them. Two example words have been given. Fill in the third one as you are sorting.

SPELLING WORDS

1. seven
2. taken
3. wagon
4. kitten
5. reason
6. certain
7. broken
8. captain
9. season
10. given
11. happen
12. kitchen

Look for other words with the same sound you hear at the end of *seven* to add to the lists. You might find *mountain* in your social studies book. You might find *frozen* or *pollen* in a weather report.

13. _____
14. _____
15. _____

mitten

bargain

▶ The ending sound you hear in *seven* can be spelled *en*, *on*, or *ain*.

142 LESSON 34 Integrated Spelling

Name _____

Strategy Workshop

SPELLING CLUES: Guessing and Checking

When you're not sure how to spell a word, make a guess. After you've tried to spell the word on your own, check a dictionary to see whether you're right.

Look at the two possible spellings. Circle the spelling you think is incorrect. Then check the correct spelling and write the word correctly.

1. taken   takon
2. givin   given
3. capten   captain
4. kitten   kittain
5. wagon   wagen

6–11. Complete the TV commercial. Write the correct spelling. If you're not sure how to spell a word, guess and check.

Hello, juice lovers. Does this ever (**6. happen, happon**) to you? You're in the (**7. kitchin, kitchen**), enjoying a glass of juice. All of a sudden—OOPS! You've got a (**8. brokain, broken**) glass and a mess to clean up! Well, here's a (**9. reason, reasen**) to be happy! Now you can buy a glass that will not break! We're so (**10. certen, certain**) you'll like it, we'll give you your money back if you don't! So order now, for only (**11. seven, sevon**) dollars. Drink up!

1. _____
2. _____
3. _____
4. _____
5. _____

6. _____
7. _____
8. _____
9. _____
10. _____
11. _____

FUN WITH WORDS Write a Spelling Word to complete the riddle.

Why did the boy stumble so often in November?
Because the __12__ was *fall*!

12. _____

Name _____

Television WORDS

newscaster
famous
television
camera

SPELLING LOG Think about how you might use these words in your writing, and add them to your Spelling Log.

1. _____
2. _____
3. _____
4. _____

Vocabulary WordShop

Would you like a job in television? Use the Television Words to complete each job description below.

Wanted: Responsible person to operate a TV __1__. Must have a steady hand. Need someone who can always "get the picture" quickly. Call 555-3479.

Want to be rich and __2__? We're looking for people of all ages to act in special commercials. No experience necessary. Call 555-0122.

Opening available: Local TV station seeks a __3__ for afternoon and evening broadcasts. Must be able to read and speak well. Call 555-0774.

Work part-time or full-time in all areas of __4__. For more information, call Station XZYP. Ask for Ms. Cast. Call 555-0044.

5–8. What other words used in television jobs can you think of? Write them on the lines at the left.

5. _____
6. _____
7. _____
8. _____

144 LESSON 34

Integrated Spelling

Name _____

WHAT'S IN A WORD?

The word *newscaster* is formed by joining the word *news* with part of the word *broadcaster*. A newscaster is someone who broadcasts, or announces, the news.

1. What is a *weathercaster*?
2. What is a *sportscaster*?

COMBINED WORDS Choose a word from the box to match each definition. Combine parts of the two underlined words to form the word.

> smog   motel   brunch   camcorder   sitcom

3. It's a meal that is eaten between the times for <u>breakfast</u> and <u>lunch</u>.

4. It's something in the air that is a combination of <u>smoke</u> and <u>fog</u>.

5. It's a <u>hotel</u> where drivers of <u>motor</u> cars stay.

6. It's a TV show that is a <u>situation</u> <u>comedy</u>.

7. It's a machine that is both a <u>camera</u> and a <u>recorder</u>.

1. _____
   _____
   _____
2. _____
   _____
   _____
3. _____
4. _____
5. _____
6. _____
7. _____

WITH A PARTNER For each Spelling Word, create a flash card with a picture clue on one side and the Spelling Word on the other. For example, you could link a picture of a saltshaker with *season* or a ship's wheel with *captain*. Exchange flash cards with a partner. Practice your spelling by studying each other's picture clues and spelling each word.

Integrated Spelling

SPELLING WORDS

1. beside
2. alive
3. belong
4. awake
5. beyond
6. between
7. alike
8. agree
9. apart
10. amount
11. behave
12. beneath

Look for other words that begin with *a* or *be* to add to the lists. You might find *ashore* or *aboard* in an article on travel. You might find *besiege* or *betray* in a story about war.

13. _____
14. _____
15. _____

Words Like *alive* and *beneath*

Each Spelling Word begins with the letters *a* or *be*. Sort the Spelling Words in a way that will help you remember them. One example word has been given. Fill in the other one as you are sorting.

ahead

▶ The letters *a* and *be* appear at the beginning of some words.

Strategy Workshop

SPELLING CLUES: Word Shapes Pay attention to the shapes of words. To remember the spelling of a word, draw its shape.

Fill in each word shape with a Spelling Word. Use the clues to help you. Then write the words on the numbered lines.

1. Remember to ▢▢▢▢▢▢ when visiting Grandma.
2. If two things are not different, they are ▢▢▢▢▢▢.
3. At school you need to be wide ▢▢▢▢▢.
4. After you join a group, you ▢▢▢▢▢▢▢ to it.
5. Things that are not close together are far ▢▢▢▢▢▢.
6. The chair is ▢▢▢▢▢▢ the desk.

1. _____
2. _____
3. _____
4. _____
5. _____
6. _____

7–11. Complete the letter. Write the correct spelling of the words in parentheses.

July 30

Dear Mom and Dad,
    Camp is **(7. biyond, beyond)** anything I expected! This is the greatest **(8. amount, ammount)** of fun I've ever had. We went hiking **(9. between, batween)** lunch and dinner yesterday. I saw a snake **(10. bineath, beneath)** a rock. I wasn't sure if it was **(11. alive, allive)** or not until it moved. Boy, did I jump!
            Love,
            Max

7. _____
8. _____
9. _____
10. _____
11. _____

FUN WITH WORDS Write a Spelling Word to complete the cartoon.

I think people are too quick to accept the opinions of others.

Oh, I __12__!

12. _____

Integrated Spelling

LESSON 35 147

Name _____

Exploration WORDS

observed
discover
ponder
experiments

SPELLING LOG Think about how you might use these words in your writing, and add them to your Spelling Log.

1. _____
2. _____
3. _____
4. _____

Vocabulary WordShop

Use the Exploration Words to complete the survey below.

Do you have what it takes to be a great scientist? Take this simple quiz to see how you rate. Circle the letter in front of your answer.

1. You are walking through a field. You __1__ a plant that you've never seen before. You
   (a) ignore the plant and keep on walking.
   (b) glance at the plant once and then leave.
   (c) take the plant back to your lab to study.

2. You are performing __2__ with different chemicals. You
   (a) pay little attention to the results.
   (b) forget to take notes as you work.
   (c) jot down exactly what happens.

3. You watch the way an animal behaves. Then you
   (a) forget about the animal.
   (b) find something else to do.
   (c) __3__ the animal's behavior.

4. You have __4__ a powerful hailstorm. After it ends, you
   (a) go to sleep.
   (b) have something to eat.
   (c) go outside to examine the hail.

Did you answer (c) to each question? Terrific! You might have what it takes to be a great scientist!

5-8. On the lines at the left, write other words that you might use in writing about a good scientist.

5. _____
6. _____
7. _____
8. _____

Name _____

WHAT'S IN A WORD?

The word *exploration* comes from the word *explore*. *Explore* is a verb, or action word, meaning "to look into or examine carefully." When the suffix *-ation* is added, the final e in *explore* is dropped. The word becomes a noun that means "the act of looking around or exploring."

1. What is an *explorer*?

-ATION CREATIONS Choose the word from the box that completes each sentence.

| decoration | location | donation |
| illustration | celebration | concentration |

2. Karen and Jim *celebrate* their birthdays. They have a _____.

3. The Smiths *donate* money. They give a _____.

4. The students *concentrate*. They have good _____.

 5. The girls *decorate* the classroom. They add a _____.

6. We *locate* the house. We find its _____.

 7. Artists *illustrate* books. They draw an _____.

WITH A PARTNER Make up book titles using as many of the Spelling Words as possible. One title might be *How to Behave When You Don't Agree*. Write your titles on a sheet of paper, and read them aloud.

1. _____
_____
_____
_____

2. _____
3. _____
4. _____
5. _____
6. _____
7. _____

Integrated Spelling   **LESSON 35**

Name _____

Practice Test

A. Read the three word groups in each item. Find the underlined word that is spelled wrong. On the answer sheet, mark the letter that is next to the misspelled word.

Example:
    A baseball <u>game</u>   B played on a <u>team</u>
    C a happy <u>croud</u>

1. A travel on the <u>rivar</u>   B cold <u>water</u>
   C large <u>number</u> of people

2. A the best <u>ever</u>   B too much <u>sugar</u>
   C paid a <u>doller</u>

3. A favorite <u>coler</u>   B do a <u>favor</u>
   C famous <u>author</u>

4. A <u>never</u> stopped   B looking <u>togethar</u>
   C <u>broken</u> mirror

5. A ate a <u>little</u>   B red <u>apple</u>
   C on the <u>tabel</u>

6. A in the <u>middle</u>   B a <u>normle</u> day
   C not <u>able</u> to

7. A the <u>final</u> word   B pop a <u>bubbal</u>
   C the king's <u>castle</u>

8. A a <u>purpal</u> grape   B add the <u>total</u>
   C too hot to <u>handle</u>

9. A <u>seven</u> days   B has <u>taken</u> the food
   C on a <u>wagain</u>

10. A lost <u>kitton</u>   B for no <u>reason</u>
    C very <u>certain</u>

EXAMPLE
  A   B   ●C

ANSWERS
1. A B C
2. A B C
3. A B C
4. A B C
5. A B C
6. A B C
7. A B C
8. A B C
9. A B C
10. A B C

Name _____

B. Read the three word groups in each item. Find the underlined word that is spelled wrong. On the answer sheet, mark the letter that is next to that word.

1. A broken glass   B capten of the team
   C seven years old

2. A givain a warning   B may happen soon
   C eating in the kitchen

3. A beside the house   B found alive
   C blong to a club

4. A fully awake   B beyond the river
   C btwean classes

5. A somewhat alike   B fully ahgree
   C torn apart

6. A figure the ahmount   B behave well
   C below the table

7. A an even numbar   B costs a dollar
   C never forgot

8. A handal the job   B read a little
   C table leg

9. A seat is taken   B black and white kitten
   C give me a reasen

10. A be certain   B bneeth a rock
    C juicy apple

ANSWERS

1. A B C
2. A B C
3. A B C
4. A B C
5. A B C
6. A B C
7. A B C
8. A B C
9. A B C
10. A B C

Integrated Spelling   LESSON 36 • REVIEW   151

Name _____

Unit 6: Writing Activities

WORDS TO WATCH FOR

feet
many
want
wish
their
things
been
playing

You Did It!

Think of something you've done that you're proud of and that was a great challenge to you. Perhaps you played in a championship ball game. Maybe you even helped save someone's life! Write a personal narrative that tells about the experience. Tell how you met your challenge and what happened.

Tips for Spelling Success

- Check the spelling of your verbs, both regular and irregular.
- You might also use some of the words at the left. Be careful how you spell them.

One in a Million

Congratulations! You have just won a million dollars! (Well, you can pretend you did!) What will you do with the money? Will you travel? Will you buy gifts for your friends and family? Will you start a book collection? Write a story that tells what you plan to do with your new fortune. Later, share your ideas with classmates. See how many different ideas your classmates have.

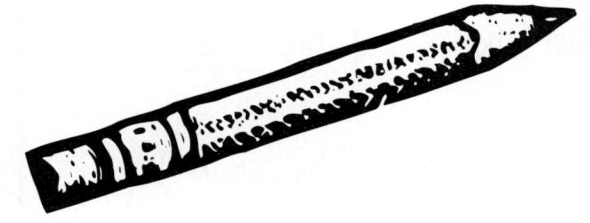

Tips for Spelling Success

- Check the spelling of adjectives you use to describe places and things.
- Use a dictionary to check any spelling you're not sure of.

152 LESSON 36 • REVIEW   Integrated Spelling

Name _____

Sell That Book!

Choose a good book that you've read lately. Create an advertisement to "sell" the book to other people. In the ad, tell what the book is about. (But don't give away the ending!) Also, give good reasons why others should read the book. Tell what's best about the story and the author's style. You can present your ad in writing or perform it as a radio or television commercial.

Tips for Spelling Success
- Proofread your book ad to make sure that all the words are spelled correctly.
- Remember, people may not buy a copy if your spelling's sloppy!

All Mixed Up!

You and a partner can have fun playing "Scrambled Words." Choose a Spelling Word. Mix up the letters. For example:

    rugas = sugar
    pleap = apple
    traap = apart

Show each scrambled word to your partner. See whether your partner can write the word correctly.

Tips for Spelling Success
- When you spell a word, think about letters that often come together, such as *qu* or *ck*.
- After you sound out your word, add any missing letters.

Integrated Spelling

Spelling Table

THE SPELLING TABLE below lists all the sounds that we use to speak the words of English. Each first column of the table gives the pronunciation symbol for a sound, such as ō. Each second column of the table gives an example of a common word in which this sound appears, such as *open* for the ō sound. Each third column of the table provides examples of the ways that a sound can be spelled, such as *oh, o, oa, ow, ough, oe,* and *o-e* for the long *o* sound.

The Sound	As In	Is Spelled As
a	**a**dd	**ca**t
ā	**a**ge	g**a**me, r**ai**n, d**ay**, p**a**per
ä	p**a**lm	**ah**, f**a**ther, d**a**rk, h**ea**rt
â(r)	c**a**re	d**are**, f**air**, b**ear**, th**eir**
b	**b**at	**b**ig, ca**b**in, ra**bb**it
ch	**ch**eck	**ch**op, mar**ch**, ca**tch**
d	**d**og	**d**ig, ba**d**, la**dd**er, calle**d**
e	**e**gg	**e**nd, m**e**t, r**ea**dy, **a**ny, s**ai**d, s**ay**s, fri**e**nd
ē	**ea**t	sh**e**, s**ee**, p**eo**ple, k**ey**, f**ie**ld, cit**y**
f	**f**it	**f**ive, o**ff**er, cou**gh**
g	**g**o	**g**ate, bi**gg**er
h	**h**ot	**h**ope, **wh**o
i	**i**t	**i**nch, h**i**t, pr**e**tty, b**ee**n, b**u**sy
ī	**i**ce	**i**tem, f**i**ne, b**uy**, tr**y**, d**ye**
j	**j**oy	**j**ump, **g**em, ma**g**ic, ca**ge**
k	**k**eep	**k**ing, **c**at, lo**ck**
l	**l**ook	**l**et, ba**ll**

154   **SPELLING TABLE**   **Integrated Spelling**

The Sound	As In	Is Spelled As
m	**m**ove	**m**ake, ha**mm**er
n	**n**ice	**n**ew, ca**n**, fu**nn**y, **kn**ow
ng	ri**ng**	thi**ng**
o	**o**dd	p**o**t, h**o**nor
ō	**o**pen	**oh**, **o**ver, g**o**, **oa**k, gr**ow**, th**ough**, t**oe**, b**o**ne
ô	d**o**g	f**o**r, m**o**re, r**oa**r, b**a**ll, w**a**lk, d**aw**n, f**au**lt, br**oa**d, **ough**t
oi	**oi**l	n**oi**se, t**oy**
o͝o	t**oo**k	f**oo**t, w**ou**ld, w**o**lf, p**u**ll
o͞o	p**oo**l	c**oo**l, l**o**se, s**ou**p
ou	**ou**t	**ou**nce, n**ow**
p	**p**ut	**p**in, ca**p**, ha**pp**y
r	**r**un	**r**ed, ca**r**, hu**rr**y
s	**s**ee	**s**it, **sc**ene, lo**ss**, li**s**ten, **c**ity
sh	ru**sh**	**sh**oe, **s**ure, o**c**ean
t	**t**op	**t**an, kep**t**, be**tt**er, walk**ed**, caugh**t**
th	**th**in	**th**ink, clo**th**
<s>th</s>	**th**is	**th**ese, clo**th**ing
u	**u**p	c**u**t, b**u**tter, s**o**me, fl**oo**d
û(r)	b**ur**n	t**ur**n, b**ir**d, w**or**k
v	**v**ery	**v**ote, o**v**er, o**f**
w	**w**in	**w**ait, to**w**el
y	**y**et	**y**ear, on**i**on
yo͞o	**u**se	**c**ue, f**ew**
z	**z**oo	**z**ebra, la**z**y, bu**zz**, wa**s**, **s**cissors
zh	vi**s**ion	gara**g**e, televi**s**ion
ə		**a**bout, list**e**n, penc**i**l, mel**o**n, circ**u**s

Spelling Dictionary

This section of your book contains your Spelling Dictionary! This is where you'll find all your Spelling Words and Vocabulary WordShop Words.

This is the entry word. It's the word you look up.

This tells you how to say it.

The letter *n.* means the entry word is a noun.

This is a sample sentence using the entry word.

There are several meanings of this entry word.

The letter *v.* means the entry word can also be a verb.

Use this key to help you figure out how the letters in a word sound.

This is the number of the lesson where you'll find the entry word.

point [*point*] *n.* **1.** a fine, sharp end: **If you break the *point* of your pencil, you'll have to sharpen it. 2.** the thought that explains the main idea or purpose of something: **The *point* of Dad's lecture was that I should keep my room cleaner. 3.** a score in a game: **The score was tied until our team scored one more *point*.** —*v.* to show the way; indicate something: **The yellow arrows *point* to the campground where we'll stay. *Point* to your favorite book.** [13]

PRONUNCIATION KEY

a	add, map	m	move, seem	u	up, done
ā	ace, rate	n	nice, tin	û(r)	burn, term
â(r)	care, air	ng	ring, song	yo͞o	fuse, few
ä	palm, father	o	odd, hot	v	vain, eve
b	bat, rub	ō	open, so	w	win, away
ch	check, catch	ô	order, jaw	y	yet, yearn
d	dog, rod	oi	oil, boy	z	zest, muse
e	end, pet	o͝o	took, full	zh	vision, pleasure
ē	equal, tree	o͞o	pool, food	ə	the schwa, an unstressed vowel representing the sound spelled **a** in *above* **e** in *sicken* **i** in *possible* **o** in *melon* **u** in *circus*
f	fit, half	ou	pout, now		
g	go, log	p	pit, stop		
h	hope, hate	r	run, poor		
i	it, give	s	see, pass		
ī	ice, write	sh	sure, rush		
j	joy, ledge	t	talk, sit		
k	cool, take	th	thin, both		
l	look, rule	th	this, bathe		

Abbreviations: *n.* noun; *v.* verb; *adj.* adjective; *adv.* adverb; *prep.* preposition; *pron.* pronoun; *interj.* interjection; *conj.* conjunction; *syn.* synonym; *poss.* possessive; *ger.* gerund

A

a·ble [āʹbəl] *adj.* having the power or skill to do something: **A flamingo is *able* to stand on one leg.** [33]

a·bove [ə·buvʹ] *prep.* higher than; over: **The roof *above* our heads protects us from the rain.** [21]

act [akt] *n.* a part of a play or show: **We were late for the play, so we missed part of the first *act*.** —*v.* to play a part in a show or movie: **Kate loves to *act* in our school plays.** [1]

a·do·be [ə·dōʹbē] *n.* as *adj.* a building block made of clay mixed with straw and dried in the sun: **When *adobe* bricks dry, the mud hardens around the straw.** [16]

a·gain [ə·genʹ] *adv.* once more; another time: **I watched the movie *again* because I wanted to see the funny parts twice.** [21]

a·go [ə·gōʹ] *adv.* in the past: **My grandma was born seventy years *ago*.** [21]

a·gree [ə·grēʹ] *v.* to have the same idea about something: **We *agree* that red is our favorite color.** [35]

a·head [ə·hedʹ] *adv.* onward; forward: **I'll get further *ahead* with my chores if I don't take a break before lunch.** [21]

air [âr] *n.* the sky; the space above the Earth: **Tom threw his ball into the *air* and caught it when it came down.** [14]

air·plane [ârʹplānʹ] *n.* a kind of vehicle that flies very fast in the air: **A jet is one kind of *airplane*.** [29]

a·like [ə·līkʹ] *adv.* like one another; similar: **Those twins look so much *alike* that I can't tell them apart.** [35]

a·live [ə·līvʹ] *adj.* having life; living: **I knew the snake was *alive* because it moved.** [35]

al·most [ôlʹmōstʹ] *adv.* very near to, but not quite: **The rain was so cold that it felt *almost* like snow.** [10]

a·lone [ə·lōnʹ] *adv.* by oneself; not with others: **Alan sat *alone* at the table and ate lunch by himself.** [21]

a·long [ə·lôngʹ] *adv.* forward: **I passed my toys *along* to my baby sister.** [21]

al·so [ôlʹsōʹ] *adv.* as well: **When we stop for sodas after the game, we'll *also* order a pizza.** [10]

al·ways [ôlʹwāz *or* ôlʹwēz] *adv.* all the time; at all times: **Mom *always* picks me up from school at 3:30.** [10]

a·mount [ə·mountʹ] *n.* a certain number or quantity: **Lupe and I each bought a large soda, so we spent the same *amount* of money.** [35]

am·phib·i·an [am·fibʹē·ən] *n.* one of a group of cold-blooded animals with backbones that can live on land and in water: **Frogs are *amphibians* because they can live on land or in water.** [21] ◆

> ◆ **Amphibian** comes from an old Greek word that means "living a double life." The idea of a "double life" is based on the fact that amphibians are able to live both on land and in the water. Most animals can live in only one or the other.

an·y [eʹnē] *adj.* one of a group; one or more: **An only child doesn't have *any* brothers or sisters.** [28]

a·part [ə·pärtʹ] *adv.* away from each other in space or time: **I miss my best friend when we are *apart*.** [35]

ap·ple [aʹpəl] *n.* a round fruit with a thin red, yellow, or green skin: **I ate my *apple* and then threw away the core.** [33]

A·pril [āʹprəl] *n.* the fourth month of the year: **April comes after March and before May.** [17]

a·ris·to·crat [ə·risʹtə·kratʹ] *n.* a person who belongs to a class of people having a very high standing in society; a person who comes from a wealthy, important family: **Most of the prince's friends were rich *aristocrats* with high ranks.** [7]

a	add	ō	open	th	thin
ā	ace	ô	order	th	this
â	care	oi	oil	zh	vision
ä	palm	o͝o	took		
e	end	o͞o	pool	ə	a in about
ē	equal	ou	out		e in listen
i	it	u	up		i in pencil
ī	ice	û(r)	burn		o in melon
o	odd	yo͞o	use		u in circus

art•work [ärt′wûrk′] *n.* the illustrations or decorations of printed books, magazines, or the like: **Alex thinks that the pictures in comic books are wonderful *artwork*.** [4]

a•sleep [ə·slēp′] *adj.* sleeping: **My dog is *asleep*, but he'll wake up if I call him.** [21]

ate [āt] *v.* the past form of *eat*. [16]

at•mo•sphere [at′mə·sfēr′] *n.* the area around the Earth that has air for breathing: **Oxygen is one component of the Earth's *atmosphere*.** [32] ◆

> ◆ **Atmosphere** means the "layer of air that surrounds the planet Earth." Because this surrounding air makes the Earth what it is, the meaning of the word *atmosphere* has taken on another meaning. It has been extended to mean "the special mood or character that something has," as in **A restaurant called Mom's Home Cookin' should have a friendly *atmosphere*.**

at•tack [ə·tak′] *v.* to set upon with force; try to injure: **The wolf *attacks* animals that are its prey.** [20]

au•thor [ô′thər] *n.* a person who writes a book, article, poem, or other such work: **Frank wrote the *author* a letter to tell her how much he enjoyed reading her newest book.** [32]

a•wake [ə·wāk′] *adj.* not asleep: **The noise of the thunder kept me *awake* most of the night.** [35]

a•ware [ə·wâr′] *adj.* taking notice of; knowing about: **I wasn't *aware* that Dad was asleep until I heard him snoring.** *syn.* realizing [14]

ax•is [ak′səs] *n.* a straight line, usually unseen, around which a body turns or seems to turn: **We can't feel the Earth turning on its *axis*.** [32]

B

ba•bies' [bā′bēz] *poss.* belonging to more than one baby: **Most *babies'* diapers need to be changed often.** [23]

ba•by's [bā′bēz] *poss.* belonging to or of a baby: **Please warm up the *baby's* bottle.** [23]

ball [bôl] *n.* a large, formal dance: **Cinderella lost her slipper after she danced with Prince Charming at the *ball*.** [7]

bear [bâr] *n.* a very large wild animal with thick fur, short legs, and sharp claws: **The mother *bear* got food for her two cubs.** [14]

bear

be•come [bi·kum′] *v.* to come to be; take on a certain state or condition: **The pudding will *become* firm after we put it in the refrigerator.** [21]

bed•room [bed′rōōm′] *n.* a room with a bed for sleeping: **I keep my piggy bank on the dresser in my *bedroom*.** [29]

be•fore [bi·fôr′] *conj.* at an earlier time than: **Eat your dinner *before* you eat your dessert.** [15]

be•gin [bi·gin′] *v.* to start: **The new year will *begin* on January 1.** [21]

be•have [bi·hāv′] *v.* to act or do in a certain way: **We *behave* nicely when we use good manners.** [35]

be•hind [bi·hīnd′] *adv.* at the back; in the rear: **She hit the other car from *behind*.** [21]

be•long [bi·lông′] *v.* to be a member of: **My brother and I *belong* to this family.** [35]

be•low [bi·lō′] *prep.* lower than; under: **Your nose is *below* your eyes and above your mouth.** [21]

be•neath [bi·nēth′] *prep.* lower than; under: **Traci's napkin fell *beneath* the table.** [35]

be•side [bi·sīd′] *prep.* at the side of; near: **Sally sat close *beside* me and whispered in my ear.** [35]

be•sides [bi·sīdz′] *prep.* in addition to: **Besides taking piano lessons, Becky also plays in recitals.** [21]

best

best [best] *adj.* better than all the others: **Ken won first prize because he had the *best* science project.** [1] ◆

◆ **Best** and **better** are used in different ways. *Best* means that something is ahead of all others: **Of all the books I have read by that author, I think the latest one is her *best* book.** If you are talking about a thing that is ahead of just one other thing, use *better*, not *best*: **Of those two books, the first one is *better*** (not "Of those two books, the first one is best").

bet•ter [be′tər] *adj.* improved in health or condition: **Daniel felt *better* after his sore throat had stopped hurting.** [26]

be•tween [bi·twēn′] *prep.* in the place or time that keeps two things apart: **February is the month *between* January and March.** [35]

be•yond [bē·änd′] *prep.* on or to the far side of: **Don't swim out to the deep water *beyond* the dock!** [35]

big [big] *adj.*, **bigger, biggest.** great in amount or size: **An ocean is *bigger* than a lake. Whales are the *biggest* creatures in the ocean.** [11]

bird [bûrd] *n.* an animal that has wings and feathers: **A parrot is a large *bird* with brightly colored feathers.** [19]

birth•day [bûrth′dā′] *n.* the day on which a person is born: **My twin sister and I have the same *birthday*.** [29]

blew [blōō] *v.* the past form of *blow*. [16]

bloom [blōōm] *n.* a blossom or flower: **After Beth planted her seeds, she waited for the first *bloom* to appear.** [27]

blos•som [blo′səm] *n.* a flower or group of flowers, especially of a tree or plant that bears fruit: **The pink cherry *blossom* is a flower with a sweet smell.** [27]

blow [blō] *v.*, **blew, blown, blowing.** to move the air; send a stream of air: **The wind *blew* my tree house down, but Dad will fix it.** [16]

blue [blōō] *adj.* the color of the sky on a clear day: **The lake was as *blue* as the sky.** [16]

bot•tom [bo′təm] *n.* the part of a thing that is opposite the top; the lowest part: **The dime sank to the *bottom* of the water, but the leaf floated on top.** [26]

bound•a•ry [boun′də·rē] *n.*, **boundaries.** the outer limit or edge of something: **My dog chases animals that cross the *boundaries* of our yard.** [20]

boy's [boiz] *poss.* belonging to one boy: **The *boy's* toys were in his bedroom.** [22]

boys' [boiz] *poss.* belonging to more than one boy: **The *boys'* uniforms got muddy when they played football in the rain.** [23]

brain [brān] *n.* the mind; intelligence: **Let's put our *brains* together to come up with a plan.** [2]

brave [brāv] *adj.* not afraid of danger: **The *brave* firefighter rescued the baby from the burning house.** [11]

bread [bred] *n.* a food made by mixing flour with a liquid and baking it in an oven: **Pam likes peanut butter and jelly sandwiches on white *bread*.** [1]

bro•ken [brō′kən] *adj.* having or showing a crack or break: **Dr. Larson put a cast on my *broken* arm.** [34]

broth•er's [bru′thərz] *poss.* belonging to or of a brother: **My *brother's* favorite poster is hanging above his bed.** [23]

brown [broun] *n.* as *adj.* a dark color like that of chocolate or mud: **Grass will turn *brown* if you don't give it enough water.** [13]

bub•ble [bu′bəl] *n.* a thin film of liquid shaped like a ball and filled with gas or air: **When you see the first *bubble*, you'll know the water is boiling.** [33]

build•ing [bil′ding] *n.* a structure with walls and a roof: **There are six apartments in the *building* where our family lives.** [13]

burst [bûrst] *n.* a sudden break or movement: **The Fourth of July fireworks exploded in a *burst* of color.** [5]

a	add	ō	open	th	thin
ā	ace	ô	order	th	this
â	care	oi	oil	zh	vision
ä	palm	o͝o	took		
e	end	o͞o	pool	ə	a in about
ē	equal	ou	out		e in listen
i	it	u	up		i in pencil
ī	ice	û(r)	burn		o in melon
o	odd	yo͞o	use		u in circus

bury

bur•y [ber´ē] *v.*, **buries, buried.** to cover up with or as if with dirt: **My dog *buried* his big bone in our backyard.** [25]

cac•tus [kak´təs] *n.* a plant with a thick green trunk and spines or bristles instead of leaves: **A *cactus* can survive in the desert because it doesn't need a lot of water.** [16]

cactus

cam•era [kam´rə] *n.* a device used in television to form a picture and send it out as an electronic signal for broadcasting: **If we had a television *camera*, we could film our own show.** [34]

can•not [ka´not *or* ka·not´] the opposite of *can;* be unable: **I *cannot* run as fast as a rabbit.** [29]

cap•tain [kap´tən] *n.* a person who is in charge of a ship: **The *captain* gave the command to set sail.** [34]

care•ful [kâr´fəl] *adj.* taking care; paying close attention: **Laurie was *careful* not to burn herself on the hot oven.** [27]

car•ry [kâr´ē] *v.*, **carries, carried.** to have with oneself: **I *carried* a snack in my backpack to eat during the game.** [25]

cas•tle [ka´səl] *n.* a very large building or group of buildings with thick walls, towers, and many rooms: **The queen sat on her throne in the *castle*.** [33]

cause [kôz] *n.* a person or thing that makes something happen: **Lightning was the *cause* of the forest fire.** [10]

cen•ter field [sen´tər fēld´] *n.* as *adj.* in baseball, the part of the outfield behind second base: **Marc made a great *centerfield* catch to win the game.** [14]

cer•tain [sûr´tən] *adj.* completely sure that something is true or right: **I am *certain* that there are twelve eggs in a dozen.** *syn.* positive [34]

chance [chans] *n.* an opportunity or occasion to do something: **Call me as soon as you get a *chance*.** [8]

cher•ry [cher´ē] *n.*, **cherries.** a small, round fruit, usually with a red skin, with a pit in the center: **We picked enough ripe red *cherries* for Mom to bake a pie.** [25]

child [chīld] *n.* a young person; a boy or girl: **My parents have one *child*, me!** [8] ◆

> ◆ **Child** is an unusual word in that the word for the plural (more than one child) is *children*, not "childs." In fact, all three of the basic words for people have unusual plurals. *Man* becomes *men*, *woman* becomes *women*, and *child* becomes *children*. All of these are very old words that were used in English in early times, when the rules for forming plurals were not as strict as they are now.

chin [chin] *n.* the bony part of the lower face: **Your *chin* is below your mouth and above your neck.** [8]

choose [chōōz] *v.* to pick from a group: **Linda was allowed to *choose* the flavor of birthday cake she wanted.** *syn.* select [8]

church [chûrch] *n.* a building for religious services: **The parking lot at the *church* was full on Sunday.** [19]

class•room [klas´rōōm´] *n.* a room in a school where classes are held: **We write on the board at the front of our *classroom*.** [29]

class's [klas´əz] *poss.* belonging to a class: **Our *class's* attendance record was the best in the school.** [23]

clean [klēn] *adj.* not dirty: **The plates we used are now dirty, but the ones in the cupboard are *clean*.** —*v.* to remove dirt and mess from something: **When my room is messy, Mom tells me to *clean* it.** [4]

cling [kling] *v.* to hold tightly to something: **The baby monkey *clings* to its mother.** [22]

clock [klok] *n.* a device that tells what time it is: **The *clock* on the wall seemed to go very slow when I was eager to leave.** [2]

close [klōz] *v.*, **closed.** to shut something that was open: **I *close* the door when I leave the room.** [3]

close — dog's

close [klōs] *adv.*, **closer, closest.** not far away in space or time; near: **Maine is *closer* to New York than it is to California.** [11]

clo•ver [klō´vər] *n.* a small plant with leaves that have three to six leaflets and white, red, or purple flower heads: **The *clover* covered the ground like grass.** [19]

col•or [ku´lər] *n.* one of the different ways that the light from something can be sensed by the eye; red, blue, yellow, green, and so on: **Let's paint our house a new *color*.** [32]

come [kum] *v.*, **came, coming.** to go or move toward a place: **Six of Sue's friends are *coming* to her slumber party.** [20]

con•fi•dent [kon´fə·dənt] *adj.* believing strongly: **I'm *confident* I'll do well on my test because I studied very hard.** [11]

con•nect [kə·nekt´] *v.* to relate to; to be in common with: **My topic *connects* with yours because we both wrote about our pets.** [17]

cook [kŏŏk] *v.* to use heat to get food ready to be eaten: **Charlie likes to *cook* spicy chili with his dad.** —*n.* a person who gets food ready to eat: **The *cook* in our school cafeteria makes lunch every day.** [9]

cook•ie [kŏŏk´ē] *n.* a small, sweet food, usually flat and thin: **Does your chocolate chip *cookie* have nuts in it?** [28]

cool [kōōl] *adj.* a little cold; not too warm: **A *cool* drink always tastes good when you're hot and thirsty.** [9]

co•op•er•ate [kō·o´pə·rāt´] *v.* to work together for some purpose: **We *cooperate* by sharing things and helping one another.** [17]

cot•ton [ko´tən] *n.* a fabric made from the fibers of a certain plant: **I like shirts made of *cotton* because they feel soft against my skin.** [26]

cou•ra•geous [kə·rā´jəs] *adj.* showing or having bravery: **The *courageous* mother bear defended her cubs from the hunters.** [11]

crack [krak] *v.* to split; break without coming completely apart: **Lightning *cracked* the tree into two parts.** [8]

cray•on [krā´on] *n.* a short stick of colored wax or chalk, used for drawing: **Everyone colored with the red *crayon*, so it was the shortest one in the box.** [28]

cry [krī] *v.*, **cries, cried.** to make a loud call; shout: **Carrie *cries*, "Hurry up!" when she wants us to run faster.** [25]

date [dāt] *n.* the certain time when something happens or will happen: **October 31 is the *date* of Halloween.** [17]

deep [dēp] *adj.* going far down from the top or from the surface: **Mom told us not to swim in water so *deep* that it is over our heads.** [4]

din•ner [di´nər] *n.* the main meal of the day, usually eaten in the evening: **Our whole family goes to Grandma's house to eat Sunday *dinner*.** [26]

dis•cov•er [dis·ku´vər] *v.* to find out about something that was not known; find for the first time: **Do you think anyone will ever *discover* a new planet?** [35] ◆

> ◆ **Discover** is made up of two word parts that actually mean "to take the cover off something" or "uncover." If you uncover a thing, it can be seen and people can tell what it is. When something is *discovered*, such as a new star in the sky, the idea is the same. To *discover* means "to see or learn about something that before was hidden or unknown."

dis•guise [dəs·gīz´] *v.*, **disguising, disguised.** to wear special clothes that hide who one really is: **Randy *disguised* himself as a pirate for the costume party.** [15]

dog's [dôgz] *poss.* belonging to one dog: **My *dog's* favorite toy is a red ball.** [23]

a	add	ō	open	th	thin
ā	ace	ô	order	th	this
â	care	oi	oil	zh	vision
ä	palm	ŏŏ	took		
e	end	ōō	pool	ə	**a** in **about**
ē	equal	ou	out		**e** in **listen**
i	it	u	up		**i** in **pencil**
ī	ice	û(r)	burn		**o** in **melon**
o	odd	yōō	use		**u** in **circus**

dol•lar [do´lər] *n.* the basic unit of money used in the United States: **Ten dimes equal one *dollar*.** [32]

down [doun] *prep.* from a higher place to a lower one: **Carlos ran *down* the steps into the basement.** [13]

draw [drô] *v.* to bring or come close: **As our birthdays *draw* closer, my friend and I will plan our parties.** [10]

dried [drīd] *adj.* having all the natural liquid removed: **Mom showed me her collection of *dried* flowers.** [25]

drink [dringk] *v.* to swallow a liquid: **If I'm thirsty, I *drink* a glass of water.** [2]

drop [drop] *n.* a decrease; a lowering of something: **The weather gets colder when there is a *drop* in the temperature.** [2]

duch•ess [du´chəs] *n.* the wife of a duke: **The *duchess* and her husband, the duke, live in a big castle.** [7]

due [dü] *adj.* expected by a certain date: **You have a project *due* next month.** [1]

dust storm [dust stôrm] *n.* a strong wind that blows dust and other matter: **Close the car windows when we drive through that *dust storm*!** [16]

E

eat [ēt] *v.,* **ate, eaten.** to have food; take in food: **Brenda *ate* waffles for breakfast.** [16]

eight [āt] *n.* the number that is one more than seven; 8: **Nine minus one equals *eight*.** [16]

eld•er [el´dər] *n.* a person who is older: **My grandpa and grandma are the *elders* of our family.** [3]

el•lipse [i·lips´] *n.* a line curved in the shape of an oval: **The shape of the Earth's orbit is an *ellipse*.** [32]

end [end] *n.* the part where something stops; the last part: **At the *end* of the play, the audience clapped.** [1]

en•joy [in·joi´] *v.* to like to do: **I *enjoy* playing soccer more than baseball.** [13]

ev•er [e´vər] *adv.* at any time: **The best trip we *ever* took was the one to the Grand Canyon.** [32]

ev•ery [ev´rē] *adj.* all of the ones in a group; each: **I brush my teeth *every* night before I go to bed.** [28]

ev•ery•thing [ev´rē·thing´] *pron.* all things: **We packed *everything* we own in boxes right before we moved.** [29]

ex•per•i•ment [ik·sper´ə·mənt] *n.* a test or trial to find something out: **In their laboratories scientists do *experiments* that we can't try at home.** [35]

ex•plore [ik·splôr´] *v.,* **exploring, explored.** to go to a new place to learn about it: **Edward's family *explored* the beach by walking along the sand.** [26]

F

face [fās] *n.* the front of the head: **Ed had a smile on his *face* when he won a prize.** [4]

fa•mous [fā´məs] *adj.* well known to many people: **If I met a *famous* movie star, I'd ask for an autograph.** [34]

fan•ta•sy [fan´tə·sē] *n.* a thing that is imagined: **Phil's favorite *fantasy* is that he will ride a dinosaur to the moon.** [5]

farm•er [fär´mər] *n.* a person whose work is growing plants or raising animals for food: **The *farmer* went out to the barn to feed his animals.** [27]

fat [fat] *adj.* having a lot of an oily substance that is formed in the body of animals, plants, and some seeds: **If we eat too much candy, we might gain weight and get *fat*.** [1]

fa•ther's [fä´thərz] *poss.* belonging to one father: **My blue eyes come from my *father's* side of our family.** [23]

fa•vor [fā´vər] *n.* a kind act that helps someone: **Would you do me a *favor* and help me pull these weeds?** [32]

field [fēld] *n.* a large, open piece of land with few or no trees: **We planted one *field* with corn and the other with hay.** [19]

fi•nal [fī´nəl] *adj.* last; after all others: **We took our *final* test on the last day of class.** [33]

find [fīnd] *v.,* **found.** to be present: **Many kinds of fish are *found* in the ocean.** [13]

finest

fin•est [fī´nəst] *adj.* best or most excellent: **The baker's chocolate cake is the *finest* I have ever eaten.** [11]

first [fûrst] *adj.* at the very beginning; above all others: **Jenny got the blue ribbon when she won *first* prize.** [19]

flow•er [flou´ər] *n.* the part of a plant that blooms: **A daffodil is a yellow *flower*.** [13]

fly [flī] *n.,* **flies.** a type of flying insect having a single pair of wings: **The horses flicked their tails to chase the *flies* away.** [25]

fog•gy [fô´gē *or* fä´gē] *adj.* misty; full of fog: **Driving is dangerous in *foggy* weather because you can't see far ahead.** [30]

fol•low [fo´lō] *v.* to come or go after: **If you go first, I'll *follow* behind you.** [26]

foot [foŏt] *n.* the part of the body at the end of the leg: **Adam knew the shoe was too small when it wouldn't fit on his *foot*.** [9]

foot•ball [foŏt´bôl´] *n.* a game played on a large field by two teams of eleven players each. The players try to get the ball over the other team's goal line to score points: **Let's go play *football* with Glenn.** [29] ◆

> ◆ *Football* may seem to be the wrong name for this game. The kicker is the only player in football who really uses his foot. But *football* began as a form of soccer, a game in which all the players use their feet to kick the ball. As time went on, American *football* became a game of running and passing, but the name *football* remained.

force [fôrs] *n.* the ability to make something move or happen: **The wind blew with such *force* that it slammed the door shut.** [15]

form [fôrm] *n.* **1.** the way a certain thing is arranged and can be seen: **For my birthday, Mom made a cake in the *form* of a dinosaur.** *syn.* shape **2.** a piece of paper with blanks to be filled in with information: **Sometimes you have to fill out a *form* to apply for a job.** —*v.* to be or make in a certain shape: **People *form* a line in front of the booth to buy movie tickets.** [15]

fort [fôrt] *n.* a strong building for defense against attack: **The soldiers kept their supplies and weapons safe in their *fort*.** [15]

goal

forth [fôrth] *adv.* forward in direction or time: **My dog ran back and *forth* in front of the door because he wanted to go out.** [15]

found [found] *v.* the past form of *find*. [13]

Fri•day [frī´dē *or* frī´dā] *n.* the sixth day of the week: ***Friday*** **is the last school day of each week.** [17]

fry [frī] *v.* as *adj.,* **fries, fried.** to cook in hot fat or oil: **The oil spatters when we make *fried* chicken.** [25]

fun•ny [fun´ē] *adj.* making someone laugh: **Margaret laughs at the *funny* cartoons on Saturday morning.** [26]

fur [fûr] *n.* the soft, hairy covering of certain animals: **Juan brushes his dog's *fur* every day.** [19]

fur•ry [fûr´ē] *adj.* having lots of thick, soft hair: **My cat Murray is soft and *furry*.** [30]

gi•ant's [jī´ənts] *poss.* belonging to a giant: **That huge mark on the ground must be a *giant's* footprint!** [22]

girl [gûrl] *n.* a female child: **That *girl* is my baby sister.** [19]

girl's [gûrlz] *poss.* belonging to one girl: **There were gold buttons on the *girl's* dress.** [22]

give [giv] *v.,* **giving, gave, given.** to present as a gift: **Have you *given* Jim a present for his birthday?** [34]

glide [glīd] *v.* to move in a smooth, easy way: **The duck's wings don't move as it *glides* slowly across the water.** [22]

goal [gōl] *n.* a thing that a person wants or aims for: **George's *goal* is to read four books before summer is over.** *syn.* purpose [3]

a	add	ō	open	th	thin
ā	ace	ô	order	th	this
â	care	oi	oil	zh	vision
ä	palm	oŏ	took		
e	end	oō	pool	ə	**a** in about
ē	equal	ou	out		**e** in listen
i	it	u	up		**i** in pencil
ī	ice	û(r)	burn		**o** in melon
o	odd	yoō	use		**u** in circus

SPELLING DICTIONARY 163

good

good [good] *adj.*, **better, best.** having the right qualities; not bad or poor: **It's a *good* thing Steve knew how to swim when he fell into the pool.** [9]

grav•i•ty [gra´və·tē] *n.* the force that pulls things toward the center of the Earth: **There is greater *gravity* on the Earth than on the moon.** [32]

gray [grā] *n.* a color that is a mixture of black and white: **Li's favorite color is *gray*.** [4]

green [grēn] *adj.* having the color of grass: **The *green* traffic light means that cars may go.** [4]

ground [ground] *v.* to hit a baseball so that it bounces or rolls along the ground: **Tim *grounded* out his last time at bat.** [14]

grow [grō] *v.* to become or make bigger: **We planted a tree and watched it *grow* taller every year.** [3]

hair [hâr] *n.* long, very thin strands that grow on the head and other parts of the body: **Willie got his *hair* cut yesterday.** [14]

hand [hand] *n.* the end of the arm, from the wrist down: **Tina put her new ring on the little finger of her left *hand*.** [1]

han•dle [han´dəl] *v.* to control or deal with something, as if holding it in the hands: **Wild horses are hard to *handle*.** [33]

hap•pen [ha´pən] *v.* to take place; come about: **How did he *happen* to fall down the steps?** [34]

hap•py [ha´pē] *adj.*, **happier, happiest.** having or showing a good feeling; pleased: **The clown's big smile made him look *happy*. I'm *happy* with a single, *happier* with a triple, but *happiest* with a home run.** [11, 28]

have [hav] *v.*, **has, had, having.** to own or hold: **I'm *having* a party next Saturday.** [20]

head [hed] *n.* the top part of the body: **Jason put his cowboy hat on his *head* before he rode the pony.** [1]

health•y [hel´thē] *adj.* having or showing good health: **Mom says that eating good foods and getting enough sleep help keep me *healthy*.** [2] ◆

holler

◆ **Healthy** means "in good health; not sick." Today people also use the word *healthy* to mean "bringing good health; helpful to one's health," as in "It is a good idea to eat *healthy* foods such as fresh fruits and vegetables." For this meaning, it is more correct to use the word *healthful*: **It is a good idea to eat *healthful* foods.**

hear [hir] *v.* to get sound through the ears; sense with the ears: **When I *hear* the phone ring, I answer it.** [16]

heav•y [he´vē] *adj.*, **heavier, heaviest.** having weight, especially great weight: **That big rock is too *heavy* for me to lift.** [28]

he'd [hēd] *cont.* a short form for *he had* or *he would*: **He'd like to stay up, but he has to go to bed.** [22]

hel•lo [hə·lō´] *n.* a word people say when they meet or greet another person: **I always say *hello* when I answer the telephone.** [26]

her [hûr] *poss. pron.* having to do with or belonging to the woman or girl that is being talked about: **Alice ate *her* apple while Art ate his.** [19]

here [hir] *adv.* in, at, or to this place: **We'll stay *here* at home instead of going out.** [16]

he•ro [hir´ō] *n.* a person admired for great courage or great deeds: **The firefighter is a *hero* for rescuing the campers from the forest fire.** [29] ◆

◆ **Hero** goes back to a very old word that meant "to watch over; look out for; protect." The idea is that a *hero* is someone who watches over or takes care of people who need help. That is why we often use the word *hero* for someone who rescues people who are in danger, as from a fire.

hol•i•day [ho´lə·dā´] *n.* a day when most people don't work and most businesses are closed in celebration of some special event: **Our family always gets together to celebrate the *holidays*.** [10]

hol•ler [ho´lər] *v.* to yell or shout: **Ricki *hollered* to his friends for help when he fell in the river.** [8]

homeland

home•land [hōm´land´] *n.* the country where a person was born or has his or her home: **I was born in Texas, so my *homeland* is the United States.** [26]

home•work [hōm´wûrk´] *n.* schoolwork that is done outside the regular class period: **Harold has to finish his *homework* before he can watch television.** [1, 29]

hop [hop] *v.,* **hopping, hopped.** to move with quick, short jumps: **The rabbits *hopped* away when they saw the coyote.** [20]

hour [our] *n.* one of the periods of time that make up a day: **An *hour* is sixty minutes.** [16]

house [hous] *n.* a building in which people live, especially a building for one family: **Our *house* has one bedroom downstairs and three upstairs.** [13]

hue [hyōō] *n.* a color, or a certain shade of a color: **Carla had crayons in every *hue* of blue.** [5]

hun•dred [hun´drəd] *n.* as *adj.* ten times ten; 100: **There are one *hundred* years in a century.** [33]

hunt [hunt] *v.* **1.** to go after wild animals in order to catch or kill them: **My uncles *hunt* deer in the forest every fall. 2.** to look hard to try to find someone or something: **I had to *hunt* all over the neighborhood for my lost bike.** [2]

hurt [hûrt] *v.* to cause pain or damage to: **Jake *hurt* his finger when he slammed it in the door.** [19]

i•cy [ī´sē] *adj.* covered with ice: **Don't slip and fall on that *icy* sidewalk!** [30]

I'd [īd] *cont.* a short form for *I had* or *I would*: ***I'd* like to drive a car, but I'm not old enough yet.** [22]

i•mag•ine [i-ma´jən] *v.* to form an idea or picture in your mind: **Close your eyes and *imagine* that you're floating on a cloud.** [5]

im•mi•grant [i´mi-grənt] *n.* a person who comes into a foreign country to live after leaving the country in which he or she was born: **Rolf is an *immigrant* to the United States from his homeland, Germany.** [30]

July

in•hab•it [in-ha´bət] *v.* to live in or on: **Animals that *inhabit* an area with lions must be on their guard.** [23]

in•ning [i´ning] *n.* one of the parts of a baseball game: **Gary won the game when he hit a home run in the ninth *inning*.** [14]

in•ter•est [in´tə-rəst *or* in´tə-rest´] *n.* a sum of money paid for the use of someone else's money: **Your money will earn *interest* if you put it in a savings account.** [33]

its [its] *poss. pron.* having to do with or belonging to some thing: **The bird sang *its* song at sunrise.** [22] ◆

it's [its] *cont.* a short form for *it is* or *it has*: **The cake is baking, so *it's* in the oven.** [22] ◆

> ◆ **Its** and **it's** look very much alike, but their meanings are different. *Its* means "belonging to some thing." *It's* is short for "it is." The word *it's* has an apostrophe (') in place of the letter *i* in *is*. Here is a sentence that uses both words to show the difference: ***It's* (it is) time to give the dog *its* dinner.**

job [job] *n.* a thing that is worked at or done: **My brother wanted a *job* after school, so he got a paper route.** [2]

jour•ney [jûr´nē] *n.* a trip, especially a long one: **We visited France and Spain during our *journey* through Europe.** [26]

joy [joi] *n.* a feeling of happiness: **Seeing flowers bloom is a *joy* for Mom.** [13]

Ju•ly [jŏŏ-lī´] *n.* the seventh month of the year: **We'll watch the fireworks on the Fourth of *July*.** [17]

a	add	ō	open	th	thin
ā	ace	ô	order	th	this
â	care	oi	oil	zh	vision
ä	palm	ŏŏ	took		
e	end	ōō	pool	ə	**a** in about
ē	equal	ou	out		**e** in listen
i	it	u	up		**i** in pencil
ī	ice	û(r)	burn		**o** in melon
o	odd	yōō	use		**u** in circus

SPELLING DICTIONARY 165

June

June [jo͞on] *n.* the sixth month of the year: **My cousin is getting married in *June*.** [17]

K

kids' [kidz] *poss.* belonging to or having to do with kids (children): ***Kids'* dinners are cheaper than adults' dinners at some restaurants.** [23]

kitch•en [ki´chən] *n.* a room in which food is cooked: **The salt and pepper are on the table in the *kitchen*.** [34]

kit•ten [ki´tən] *n.* a young cat: **My cat is sleeping beside her new *kitten*.** [34]

knap•sack [nap´sak´] *n.* a canvas or leather bag used to carry clothes, camping equipment, and so on: **I carry my lunch and my books to school in my *knapsack*.** [28]

knee [nē] *n.* the joint of the leg between the thigh and the lower leg, or the area around this joint: **Erin got down on her hands and *knees* to look under the bed.** [7]

knew [no͞o] *v.* the past form of *know*. [7]

knife [nīf] *n.* a tool that has a sharp blade in a handle and is used for cutting or as a weapon: **Wendy cut an apple with a *knife*.** [7]

knock [nok] *v.* to hit something with a loud, hard blow: **Jody had to *knock* on Joe's door because his doorbell was broken. The mailman *knocked* on our door to deliver the package.** [7, 15]

know [nō] *v.,* **knew, known.** to have in the mind; learn the truth or facts about: **I *know* that the sun rises every morning. Keiko *knew* where her brother was hiding because she heard him laughing. If I had *known* all the answers, I would have gotten an "A" on the test.** [3, 7]

L

la•dy [lā´dē] *n.,* **ladies.** woman: **The announcer said, "*Ladies* and gentlemen, may I have your attention?"** [25]

locker

large [lärj] *adj.* great in size or amount; not small: **The *large* pizza is big enough for our whole family.** [14]

latch [lach] *v.* to fasten a door or gate, using a device that holds it shut: ***Latch* the gate to make sure the pony can't get out.** [15]

laugh [laf] *v.* to make sounds that show you are happy or amused: **We'll all *laugh* if you tell a funny joke.** [7]

lead•er [lē´dər] *n.* a person who is at the head or front; a person who leads: **The *leader* of our scout troop taught us to tie square knots.** [27]

lease [lēs] *v.* to rent or use by means of a written agreement: **Dad will *lease* our apartment for one year.** [13]

leave [lēv] *v.,* **leaving, left.** to go away from a place: **Tommy felt sick, so he *left* the party and went home.** [1]

left [left] *adj.* the opposite of *right*: **The driver sits on the *left* side of the school bus.** —*v.* the past form of *leave*: **His bus *left* before he got to the bus stop.** [1]

les•son [le´sən] *n.* a thing to be learned; a part of a course of study: **We learn twelve spelling words in each of our spelling *lessons*.** [25]

let [let] *v.,* **letting.** allow or permit: **Mom says she'll think about *letting* me spend the weekend at Grandma's house.** [20]

library [lī´brer´ē] *n.* a place in which books, magazines, and other reference materials are kept for use, not for sale: **I checked out books about dinosaurs at the *library*.** [1]

lie [lī] *v.* **1.** to be in a flat position on a surface: **Doug's dog likes to *lie* by the fire and sleep.** **2.** to tell something that is not true: **Mom says it's always better to tell the truth than to *lie*.** —*n.* something that a person says, knowing it is not true: **Alice told a *lie* when she said my skates were hers.** [3]

lit•tle [li´təl] *n.* a small amount: **I sip hot cocoa slowly, a *little* at a time.** [33]

lock•er [lo´kər] *n.* as *adj.* a small closet or cabinet that can be locked, used to store personal items in a public place: **I'll give Liza my *locker* combination so she can bring my books home.** [28]

lone•ly [lōn´lē] *adj.* unhappy about being alone: **Pat felt *lonely* when her friends went to camp and she stayed home.** [27]

long [lông] *adj.,* **longer. 1.** being a great distance or amount from one end to the other: **A giraffe has a *long* neck. 2.** lasting a certain amount of time: **A week is *longer* than a day.** [10, 11]

loose [lōos] *adj.* not fastened or held tight: **My bike shook when I rode it because my back tire was *loose*.** [9] ◆

◆ **Loose** and **lose** are two words that people sometimes mix up. They write "I couldn't find that library book. I am sorry for *loosing* it." What they really mean to write is "I am sorry for *losing* it."

---

lost [lôst] *adj.* missing; not found: **Dad can't read his book until he finds his *lost* glasses.** *syn.* missing [10]

loud [loud] *adj.* having a strong sound; making noise: **The band's music was so *loud* that we could hear it from down the block.** [13]

mam•mal [ma´məl] *n.* the name used in science for an animal that has a backbone, is warm-blooded, and has hair or fur on the body: **You can tell a whale is a *mammal* because it has hair and its babies drink milk.** [21]

March [märch] *n.* the third month of the year: **Some people say *March* comes in like a lion and goes out like a lamb.** [17]

mark [märk] *n.* a spot or impression on a thing: **Dave made his *mark* on the team when he scored the winning goal.** [14]

mar•ry [mâr´ē] *v.,* **marries, married.** to become a person's husband or wife: **My dad *married* my mom fifteen years ago.** [25]

May [mā] *n.* the fifth month of the year: ***May* is the month that comes before June.** [17]

may•or [mā´ər] *n.* a person who is elected as the head of a city or town: **Our *mayor* runs our city's government from her office in City Hall.** [3]

mead•ow [me´dō] *n.* a large area of grassy land: **Grandpa's cows graze in the *meadow* near the barn.** [19]

meet [mēt] *v.* to come face to face with: **Did you ever *meet* a baseball star and get an autograph?** [4]

men's [menz] *poss.* belonging to or for men: **The *men's* clothing department is next to the boys' department.** [23]

mid•dle [mi´dəl] *n.* a place or position at or near the center: **Jessica is standing in the *middle*, between her two brothers.** [33]

mi•gra•tion [mī·grā´shən] *n.* the act of moving from one place to live in another because of certain problems or conditions: **Great-grandma was part of a *migration* of Swedes who settled in Wisconsin.** [30]

mil•lion [mil´yən] *adj.* the number that is 1,000 times 1,000; 1,000,000: **A millionaire is a person who has at least one *million* dollars.** [33]

mir•ror [mir´ər] *n.* a smooth, shiny surface that shows the image of whatever is in front of it: **Dad looks in the *mirror* when he shaves.** [32]

Mon•day [mun´dē *or* mun´dā] *n.* the second day of the week: **After a weekend of rest, Dad goes back to work on *Monday*.** [17]

mon•ey [mun´ē] *n.* the coins and paper bills that are worth a certain amount and that are used to pay for things: **I saved enough *money* to buy a hamster.** [28]

moon [mōon] *n.* the large heavenly body that can be easily seen from the Earth at night: **Astronaut Neil Armstrong was the first person to walk on the *moon*.** [9]

a	add	ō	open	th	thin
ā	ace	ô	order	th	this
â	care	oi	oil	zh	vision
ä	palm	ŏŏ	took		
e	end	ōō	pool	ə	a in about
ē	equal	ou	out		e in listen
i	it	u	up		i in pencil
ī	ice	û(r)	burn		o in melon
o	odd	yōō	use		u in circus

SPELLING DICTIONARY 167

moth•er's [muˊt͟hərz] *poss.* belonging to or of a mother: **I call my** *mother's* **sister Aunt Suzanne.** [23]

move [mo͞ov] *v.,* **moving, moved.** to change the place where one lives: **I missed my best friend after she** *moved* **away.** [20]

mov•ie [mo͞oˊvē] *n. as adj.* a show in which a series of many pictures on a film appear to move when they are shown on a screen: **When the new** *movie* **theater opened, they gave away free popcorn.** [28]

much [much] *adv.* to a great extent: *Much* **to my surprise, the party was for me!** [8]

mud•dy [muˊdē] *adj.* covered with dirt that is wet, soft, and sticky: **My dog got her feet** *muddy* **by walking in the wet field.** [30]

N

nap [nap] *n.* a short sleep: **If I'm sleepy in the afternoon, I take a** *nap.* [1]

nev•er [neˊvər] *adv.* not at any time; not ever: **I'll** *never* **tell anyone your secret.** [32]

news•cast•er [no͞ozˊkasˊtər] *n.* a person who presents the news on a radio or television show: **The** *newscaster* **reported the results of the election.** [34] ◆

◆ **Newscaster** is a new word that comes from the word *broadcaster.* To *broadcast* something is to send it out over a wide area. The idea is that a TV newscaster *casts* (sends) the *news* out over a wide area, to many people.

next [nekst] *adv.* coming or being near in time or place: **First, cut the wood into three pieces;** *next,* **paint it blue.** [1]

nice [nīs] *adj.,* **nicer, nicest.** pleasing or good in some way, as by being kind, friendly, well done, or well made: **Brad's brand-new tennis shoes are** *nicer* **than his old dirty ones. Kathy is the** *nicest* **girl in our class because she is so friendly to everyone.** [11]

noon [no͞on] *n.* the middle of the day; twelve o'clock in the daytime: **Rachel is always hungry at** *noon,* **when it's time to eat lunch.** [9]

nor•mal [nôrˊməl] *adj.* just as it should be; healthy and natural: **My temperature is a** *normal* **98.6 degrees.** [33]

nos•y [nōˊzē] *adj.* concerned with things that are not one's business: **Our** *nosy* **neighbor peeks over the fence into our yard.** [30]

num•ber [numˊbər] *n.* a symbol or word that tells how many: **Six is an even** *number.* [32]

O

ob•serve [əb·zûrvˊ] *v.,* **observing, observed.** to watch carefully for a special purpose: **The astronomer** *observed* **the stars through his telescope.** [35]

of•fice [ôˊfəs] *n.* a building or room where the work of a business is done: **I went to work with Dad and sat at the desk in his** *office.* [13]

oil [oil] *n.* **1.** a heavy, dark liquid that is found beneath the Earth's surface and that is used to make gasoline and other fuels: **Gasoline is made from** *oil.* **2.** any of various other thick, greasy substances that will float on water and burn easily: **Mom fries vegetables in olive** *oil.* [13]

one [wun] *n.* the number that is greater than zero and less than two; 1: **I ate** *one* **of my cookies and saved the others.** [16]

our [our] *poss. pron.* of or belonging to us: **We keep a lot of junk in** *our* **garage.** [16]

out [out] *adv.* away from the inside: **Martin's money fell** *out* **of the hole in his pocket.** [13]

out•side [outˊsīdˊ *or* outˊsīdˊ] *adv.* outdoors: **Lynn likes to play** *outside* **in her backyard.** [29]

own•er [ōˊnər] *n.* a person who owns a thing: **The** *owner* **of a pet must keep it safe and feed it every day.** [27]

pageant

pag•eant [pa´jənt] *n.* a play or show about some event in the past: **We'll dress up like the Pilgrims for our school's Thanksgiving** *pageant.* [10]

paint [pānt] *n.* a mixture of a coloring material and water, oil, or some other liquid: **I always use red** *paint* **when I am painting my house.** [4]

pal•ace [pa´ləs] *n.* a huge building in which a king or other ruler lives: **The prince's** *palace* **had fifty huge rooms and a beautiful throne.** [7]

part•ner [pärt´nər] *n.* a person who does something with another person: **Choose a** *partner* **for the next dance.** [17]

par•ty [pär´tē] *n.* a time when people get together to have fun or to celebrate something: **Ed invited eleven friends to his birthday** *party.* [28]

paw [pô] *n.* any of the feet of a four-footed animal, such as a dog or cat: **Kate's kitten has two white** *paws* **in front and two gray ones in back.** [10]

peach [pēch] *n.*, **peaches.** a sweet, juicy fruit with a fuzzy skin and a hard pit: **I'd rather have a** *peach* **than a plum because a peach tastes sweeter.** [8]

per•son [pûr´sən] *n.* a man, woman, or child: **A human being is a** *person.* [19]

pet•al [pe´təl] *n.* one of the parts of a flower: **When all of its** *petals* **opened, the rose was as big as a saucer.** [27]

phone [fōn] *n.* an electronic device that is used to talk to people far away; a telephone: **I couldn't visit Jerry in the hospital, but I called him on the** *phone.* [7]

phys•i•cal [fi´zi·kəl] *adj.* having to do with solid, material things, such as the body: **Pete's biggest** *physical* **change over the summer was that he grew an inch.** [2]

pick [pik] *v.* to take up with the hands; gather: **We** *picked* **blackberries from the bushes.** [20]

pi•ña•ta [pēn·yä´tə] *n.* a decorated container filled with toys and candy that hangs from the ceiling and is broken with a stick held by a blindfolded child. **When Pilar broke the** *piñata,* **candy fell down all around.** [10] ◆

◆ **Piñata** is a word that came into the English language from Spanish. This is why it is spelled with the letter ñ, which is *n* with a tilde (˜) over it. This letter is spoken as an /n/ sound followed by a /y/ sound. The breaking of a *piñata* is a custom at children's parties in Latin American countries such as Mexico, and now many children in the United States also do this at parties.

---

play•er [plā´ər] *n.* a person who plays a game or sport: **A football** *player* **wears a helmet for protection during games.** [27]

play•ful [plā´fəl] *adj.* full of fun; wanting to play: **My cat is so** *playful* **that she'll push a ball of yarn around for hours.** [27]

play•ground [plā´ground´] *n.* an outdoor area where young children can play: **The big swings are my favorite things on our** *playground.* [29]

pod [pod] *n.* a plant part that is a shell or case in which seeds grow: **One** *pod* **can contain enough seeds to grow many flowers.** [27]

point [point] *n.* **1.** a fine, sharp end: **If you break the** *point* **of your pencil, you'll have to sharpen it. 2.** the thought that explains the main idea or purpose of something: **The** *point* **of Dad's lecture was that I should keep my room cleaner. 3.** a score in a game: **The score was tied until our team scored one more** *point.* —*v.* to show the way; indicate something: **The yellow arrows** *point* **to the campground where we'll stay.** *Point* **to your favorite book.** [13]

a	add	ō	open	th	thin
ā	ace	ô	order	<u>th</u>	this
â	care	oi	oil	zh	vision
ä	palm	ŏŏ	took		
e	end	ōō	pool	ə	**a** in about
ē	equal	ou	out		**e** in listen
i	it	u	up		**i** in pencil
ī	ice	û(r)	burn		**o** in melon
o	odd	yōō	use		**u** in circus

Integrated Spelling   **SPELLING DICTIONARY**   **169**

pon•der [pon´dər] *v.* to think about a thing very seriously: I'll *ponder* all the facts before I make a decision. [35]

pos•i•tive [po´zə·tiv] *adj.* absolutely sure; with no doubt: Pam's *positive* attitude makes her feel she can learn anything. [11]

pred•a•tor [pre´də·tər] *n.* an animal that lives by hunting other animals for food: A hawk is a *predator* that spots its prey from the sky. [23]

pre•tend [pri·tend´] *v.* to act as if something is true or real when it is not; make-believe: I hid behind the curtain and *pretended* I wasn't in my room. [15]

pret•ty [pri´tē] *adj.* nice to look at; pleasing to the eyes: Mom looks *pretty* when she fixes her hair and puts on a party dress. [28]

prey [prā] *n.* an animal that is hunted by another animal for food: Wolves hunt *prey* such as rabbits and other small mammals. [20]

proud [proud] *adj.* feeling good about something you have done or that relates to you: I'm *proud* of Grandpa because people respect him and ask for his advice. [29]

pull [pŏol] *v.* to hold something and move it along with oneself: Mom *pulled* down the shades before she went to bed. [20]

pup•py [pu´pē] *n.*, **puppies.** a young dog: Jon's dog had a litter of seven *puppies*. [25] ◆

◆ **Puppy** goes back to the Latin word *pupa*, which means "a little girl" or "a doll." We get several words that refer to young or small things from this, such as *puppet* and *pupil* as well as *puppy*. The word *pupa* itself is also now used in English. It means an early stage in the life of an insect.

puppy

pur•ple [pûr´pəl] *adj.* having the color made by mixing red and blue together: Lilacs are *purple* flowers. [33]

push [pŏosh] *v.* to press on something in order to move it: The men helped Dad *push* the car to get it started. [8]

Q

quick•ly [kwik´lē] *adv.* rapidly, or in a fast way: The mouse ran *quickly* into its hole when the cat chased it. [27]

R

rain•y [rā´nē] *adj.* having a lot of rain: You'll get wet if you go outside on a *rainy* day. [30]

raise [rāz] *v.*, **raising, raised. 1.** to move to a higher place or position: I *raise* my hand when I know the answer in class. **2.** to bring up and take care of: Paul got his pony from a farm where they *raise* horses. —*n.* an increase in the amount of a worker's pay: Tony's dad earned more money after he got a *raise* of $50 a week. [4]

real [rēl] *adj.* not imagined or made up: I have a model plane, but someday I'd like to fly in a *real* jet. *syn.* true [4]

re•al•ly [rē´ə·lē *or* rē´lē] *adv.* very much; very: I *really* meant it when I said I was sorry. [27]

rea•son [rē´zən] *n.* a fact that explains why something happens as it does: My *reason* for being late is that my car had a flat tire. [34]

re•cess [rē´ses] *n.* a time when work stops: When *recess* is over, we stop playing games and go back to class. [25]

re-en•er•gize [rē·en´ər·jīz´] *v.*, **re-energizing, re-energized.** to make strong again: My body *re-energizes* itself when I take a nap. [2]

rehearsal

re•hears•al [ri·hûrʹsəl] *n.* a practice session before a final performance: **We have two more *rehearsals* before the school play.** [10]

rent [rent] *v.* to have or give the right to use something in exchange for money: **We *rent* our apartment from our landlord, Mr. Simms, who owns the building.** [13]

rep•tile [repʹtīl] *n.* any of a large group of cold-blooded animals that have backbones and dry, scaly skin: **Rattlesnakes are dangerous *reptiles*.** [21]

rich [rich] *adj.,* **richer, richest.** having much money, property, or other valuable things: **If I'm poorer than you are, then you're *richer* than I am. The *richest* person in the world has more money than anyone else.** [11]

ring [ring] *n.* a circle that is open in the center: **We sat in a *ring* around the campfire, toasting marshmallows.** [2]

rise [rīz] *v.* to move from a lower to a higher place; go up: **During the flood, Fred saw the water *rise* above the riverbanks.** [3]

riv•er [riʹvər] *n.* a large, natural stream of moving freshwater that goes into a lake, ocean, or other larger body of water: **We'll cross the bridge to get to the other side of the *river*.** [32]

ro•dent [rōʹdənt] *n.* as *adj.* one of a large family of animals with large, sharp front teeth used for gnawing: **Dad put down a *rodent* trap in the basement.** [21] ◆

> ◆ **Rodent** comes from a word meaning "to gnaw" or "to chew." These animals, such as mice, rats, beavers, and squirrels, are known for their large, strong front teeth.

rough [ruf] *adj.* not smooth or even: **My dad's face feels *rough* when he doesn't shave.** [7]

rum•ble [rumʹbəl] *n.,* **rumbled, rumbling.** a deep, heaving, rolling sound: **Being nervous or hungry can cause a *rumbling* in your stomach.** [9]

run•ning [ruʹning] *ger.* the act of going by moving the legs quickly: **Greg bought new athletic shoes for *running* on the track.** [20]

season

salt•y [sôlʹtē] *adj.* having a lot of salt: **Pretzels and potato chips are *salty*.** [30]

same [sām] *adj.* like another in every way: **Beth and I got the *same* grade on the last math test—we both got an 87.** [4]

sand•y [sanʹdē] *adj.* covered with sand: **Our towels are all *sandy* from our trip to the beach.** [30]

save [sāv] *v.,* **saving, saved.** to make free from harm or danger: **The lifeguard *saved* the boy from drowning.** [20]

scat•ter [skaʹtər] *v.* to go or cause to go in different directions: **The wind will *scatter* the fallen leaves all over our yard.** [26]

scene [sēn] *n.* the place where something happens: **The police arrived at the *scene* of the crime.** *syn.* location [16]

scoop [skoop] *v.* to take something with a bowl-shaped tool: **Help me *scoop* up sand into this pail.** [9]

scratch [skrach] *v.,* **scratches.** to rub or scrape the skin when it itches: **Art's arm itched, so he started to *scratch* it.** [5]

scream [skrēm] *v.* to cry out with a sudden, loud, and high sound: **Did you hear Mrs. Myers *scream* when she saw the mouse?** [5]

screen [skrēn] *n.* **1.** a frame holding a wire netting, used in a door or window to keep out insects: **The *screen* on our front door lets air in but keeps bugs out. 2.** a flat surface that reflects light, used to show movies or slides: **We watched the movie on the big *screen* at the theater.** [5]

sea•son [sēʹzən] *n.* one of the four parts of the year; winter, spring, summer, or fall: **Spring is the *season* right before summer.** [34]

a	add	ō	open	th	thin
ā	ace	ô	order	th	this
â	care	oi	oil	zh	vision
ä	palm	ŏŏ	took		
e	end	ōō	pool	ə	**a** in about
ē	equal	ou	out		**e** in listen
i	it	u	up		**i** in pencil
ī	ice	û(r)	burn		**o** in melon
o	odd	yōō	use		**u** in circus

see [sē] *v.,* **saw, seen.** to look at; sense with the eyes: **I've *seen* you checking out books at the library.** [16]

set•tler [set′lər] *n.* a person who goes to live in a new area or country, especially one who is among the first to live there: **A *settler* often had to build a house with whatever materials were nearby.** [30]

sev•en [se′vən] *adj.* the number that is one more than six; 7: **Sandra is *seven* years old now, but last year she was six.** [34]

shake [shāk] *v.* to make a series of small, quick body movements: **My puppy started to *shake* with fear when I took him to the vet.** [9]

share [shâr] *v.,* **sharing, shared.** to have or use a thing with another or others: **I *share* my toys with my younger brother so he can learn to play.** [14]

sharp [shärp] *adj.* having a strong and piercing sound: **When I heard his *sharp* bark, I knew I had stepped on my puppy's tail.** [8]

she'd [shēd] *cont.* a short form for *she had* or *she would:* **Angela said *she'd* feed my goldfish when I visit Grandma.** [22]

shin•y [shī′nē] *adj.* bright and shining: **New pennies are as *shiny* as glass.** [30]

shoe [shoō] *n.* an outer covering worn on the foot: **I put on my right *shoe* after I put on my socks.** [9]

shook [shŏŏk] *v.* moved back and forth with short, quick movements: **Richard *shook* his head "no."** [8]

shop [shop] *v.,* **shopping, shopped.** to visit stores to look at or buy goods: **Mom and I *shopped* for my new school clothes.** [20]

shut [shut] *v.* to stop the operation or activity of something: **Tonya *shut* off the television when the cartoons were over.** [2]

side•walk [sīd′wôk′] *n.* an area to walk along the side of a road: **We walked down the *sidewalk* and looked in all the store windows.** [29]

sight [sīt] *n.* **1.** the power to see: **We all lose our *sight* when we close our eyes. 2.** a thing to see: **The two shooting stars crossing the sky were quite a *sight*. Nancy's favorite *sight* in New York City is the Statue of Liberty.** [3]

sin•gle [sing′gəl] *v.,* **singled.** in baseball, to hit and get to first base: **The batter who *singled* was safe at first base.** [14]

sis•ters' [sis′tərz] *poss.* belonging to or of more than one sister: **My *sisters'* bedrooms are both across the hall from mine.** [23]

sketch [skech] *v.* to quickly make a drawing: **I took my pad and pencil and *sketched* a picture of my puppy.** [4] ◆

◆ **Sketch** goes back to an old word meaning "sudden" or "quick." The idea is that a *sketch* is done in a short time, usually with quick strokes of a pencil or crayon. A *sketch* is often done by an artist as the first step in creating a painting that takes longer and has much more detail.

skim [skim] *v.* to glide or move swiftly over a surface: **The dragonfly sails down, and its wings lightly *skim* the pond's surface.** [22]

sleep•y [slē′pē] *adj.* tired and needing to sleep: **I'm too *sleepy* to stay awake for the late movie.** [30]

slow•ly [slō′lē] *adv.* not fast or quick: **The turtle crawled *slowly* across the sand toward the water.** [27]

small [smôl] *adj.,* **smaller.** not having great size; not large: **I got a *small* ice cream cone with just one scoop. Three is a *smaller* number than four.** [10, 11]

soap [sōp] *n.* a substance used for washing and cleaning: **Sarah washed her face with *soap* and water.** [3]

soft [sôft] *adv.* not loud: **I spoke in a *soft* voice so I wouldn't wake up the baby.** [10]

soil [soil] *n.* the loose, top part of the ground in which plants grow: **We planted our seeds in the *soil* and then waited for them to grow.** [13]

some•one [sum′wun′] *pron.* some person who is not known or named; somebody: ***Someone* sent me a funny valentine card signed, "Your Secret Pal."** [29]

sor•ry [sôr′ē] *adj.* feeling regret or shame over something one has done: **I'm *sorry* I stepped on your foot.** [28]

soup [soōp] *n.* a liquid food made by cooking meat, fish, or vegetables in water or another liquid: **Mom always makes chicken *soup* for me when I'm sick.** [9]

southwestern

south•west•ern [south′wes′tərn] *adj.* in the direction between south and west: **Arizona and New Mexico are two of the** *southwestern* **states.** [16]

spe•cial [spe′shəl] *adj.* not like others; unusual in some way: **The Sunday my baby brother was born was a** *special* **day for our family.** [29]

sport [spôrt] *n.* a game in which people use the body, follow certain rules, and play against others to win: **Soccer is a very popular** *sport* **in Europe.** [15]

spot [spot] *n.* **1.** a mark left by dirt, food, paint, or other things: **Maria spilled the mustard and got a yellow** *spot* **on her dress. 2.** a small part that looks different from what is around it: **Mom knew I had the measles when she saw the first red** *spot* **on my face. 3.** a certain place: **My cat's favorite place to sleep is this warm** *spot* **by the fireplace.** [2]

spray [sprā] *v.* to cause to fall in tiny drops: **To color our mural, we're going to** *spray* **the paint from these cans.** [5]

spread [spred] *v.,* **spread.** to open wide or stretch open: **The girls** *spread* **a blanket out on the grass for their picnic.** [5]

sprout [sprout] *v.* to start to grow: **When seeds** *sprout,* **you see little green plants sticking out of the ground.** [5]

square [skwâr] *n.* a figure with four equal sides and angles: **The cabin by the lake is in the shape of a** *square.* [14]

stare [stâr] *v.* to look long or hard with wide-open eyes: **I** *stare* **at the beautiful colors in the sunset until they disappear.** [14]

steam•ship [stēm′ship′] *n.* a steam-powered ship that sails on the open sea: **It takes much longer to go across the ocean sailing on a** *steamship* **than it does flying on an airplane.** [26]

stick•y [sti′kē] *adj.* causing things to stick: **Wipe that** *sticky* **syrup off the counter.** [30]

still [stil] *adv.* as before; even now: **We can't have dessert yet because Dad is** *still* **eating his dinner.** [2]

stone [stōn] *n.* a single piece of the hard material that rocks are made of: **When Pedro walked along the rocky path, he got a little** *stone* **in his shoe.** [3]

study

store [stôr] *n.* a place where things are sold: **We buy our food at the grocery** *store.* [15]

sto•ry [stôr′ē] *n.* a telling of something that happens: **At the end of the** *story,* **the hero lived happily ever after.** [1, 15]

strange [strānj] *adj.* not usual or familiar; not known: **My dog barked at the** *strange* **noise he had never heard before.** [5]

street [strēt] *n.* a public road in a city or town, usually having sidewalks and buildings on either side: **My friend José lives across the** *street* **from me.** [5]

strike [strīk] *v.,* **struck, stricken.** to hit with force: **Dad will** *strike* **the dead tree with an axe to chop it down.** —*n.* in baseball, a pitch that counts against the batter, either because he or she swings and misses it, because he or she hits it foul, or because it goes over home plate: **The batter was out after his third** *strike.* [5]

string [string] *n.* a thin piece of twisted thread or wire: **Hannah held on tight to the** *string* **of her kite.** [5]

strong [strông] *adj.* **1.** having a lot of power or energy; full of strength: **The weight lifter was** *strong* **enough to lift 300 pounds.** *syn.* powerful **2.** not easily moved or changed: **The lawyer had a** *strong* **belief that his client was not guilty.** [5]

stu•dent [stoo′dənt] *n.* a person who goes to a school, college, or the like: **All the** *students* **in our school have to be in class by eight o'clock.** [25]

stu•di•o [stoo′dē-ō] *n.* a place where an artist works: **My Aunt Julia is an artist, and she painted my portrait at her art** *studio.* [4]

study [stu′dē] *v.,* **studies, studied.** to try to learn, know, or understand something by reading and thinking about it: **John** *studied* **two hours last night.** [25]

a	add	ō	open	th	thin
ā	ace	ô	order	th	this
â	care	oi	oil	zh	vision
ä	palm	o͝o	took		
e	end	o͞o	pool	ə	**a** in about
ē	equal	ou	out		**e** in listen
i	it	u	up		**i** in pencil
ī	ice	û(r)	burn		**o** in melon
o	odd	yo͞o	use		**u** in circus

Integrated Spelling   **SPELLING DICTIONARY**

such [such] *adj.* of the kind just mentioned: **Cathy likes some vegetables, *such* as corn and carrots.** [2]

sug•ar [shŏŏg´ər] *n.* a sweet substance that comes from certain plants and that is made into fine white crystals or powder: **The *sugar* in the cake makes it taste sweet.** [32]

sum•mer [su´mər] *n.* the season that comes between the spring and the fall: **I'm looking forward to our vacation this *summer*.** [17]

Sun•day [sun´dē *or* sun´dā´] *n.* the first day of the week: ***Sunday* is the second day of the weekend.** [17]

sup•per [su´pər] *n.* a meal eaten at night or in the evening: **My family and I eat *supper* at six o'clock.** [26]

sup•ply [sə·plī´] *n.*, **supplies.** an amount of something ready to be used: **Before I paint, I lay out my paper, my paints, and my other art *supplies*.** [4]

sweat [swet] *n.* a salty liquid given off through the skin: **My shirt was soaked with *sweat* after I ran two miles.** [9]

swoop [swoop] *v.* to move or go down suddenly and quickly, with a sweeping motion: **Eagles *swoop* down from the sky to catch their prey.** [22]

T

ta•ble [tā´bəl] *n.* a piece of furniture with a flat top on one or more legs: **We'll set the *table* with Mom's new dishes.** [33]

take [tāk] *v.*, **taken, taking, took. 1.** to get possession of: **We had *taken* our seats in the bleachers just before the game started. 2.** to carry: **I'm *taking* my umbrella with me in case it rains.** [20, 34]

talk [tôk] *v.* to speak about a certain subject: **Let's *talk* about everything that happened this summer at camp.** [10]

taught [tôt] *v.* the past form of *teach*.

teach [tēch] *v.*, **taught.** to cause a person to know something; give knowledge: **Our teacher *taught* us arithmetic every morning.** [25]

teach•er's [tē´chərz] *poss.* belonging to or of a teacher: **The *teacher's* ruler is on her desk.** [22]

teach•ers' [tē´chərz] *poss.* belonging to or of more than one teacher: **The *teachers'* meeting was held after school so they could all attend.** [23]

tel•e•phone [te´lə·fōn´] *n.* an electronic instrument that is used to talk to people who are far away: **I used Aunt Jean's *telephone* to call Dad to come and pick me up.**—*v.* to call someone by using a telephone: **If I have to stay late at school, I *telephone* Mom so she won't worry.** [7] ◆

> ◆ *Telephone* comes from two old words that mean "far" and "sound." The idea is that you can use a *telephone* to hear the sound of a person's voice from far away. Some other words that are formed in the same way are *telegraph* ("far writing"), *telescope* ("far seeing"), and *television* ("far vision").

tel•e•vi•sion [te´lə·vizh´ən] *n.* a system of sending pictures and sounds through the air electronically; the industry of television: **Mom lets me watch *television* when I finish my homework.** [34] ◆

tell [tel] *v.* to make known by words; say or write: **Dad will *tell* us a story before we go to sleep.** [1]

ter•ri•to•ry [ter´ə·tôr´ē] *n.* an area of land: **Wolves feel safest when they are on their own *territory*.** [20]

thank•ful [thangk´fəl] *adj.* feeling or showing thanks: **The Pilgrims were *thankful* for their good harvest.** *syn.* grateful [27]

there [t͟hâr] *adv.* at that place: **I hope you'll be *there* to see us play our last game of the season.** [14]

these [t͟hēz] *adj.* the ones that are here or nearer: ***These* flowers are yellow, but those over there are blue.** [4]

they've [t͟hāv] *cont.* a short form for *they have*: **Our neighbors aren't here, because *they've* gone on vacation.** [22]

thick•et [thi´kət] *n.* a group of bushes or small trees growing close together: **The fox hid her babies under a bush in the *thicket* to protect them.** [19]

thin [thin] *adj.*, **thinner, thinnest.** not having much body weight; not fat: **If you're fatter than I am, then I'm *thinner* than you are.** [11]

think [thingk] *v.* to have a certain idea or opinion: **We *think* that multiplication is harder than division.** [2]

third [thûrd] *adj.* next after second: **If you hit a triple in baseball, you run to *third* base.** [19]

thou•sand [thou′zənd] *n.* as *adj.* the number that is ten times one hundred; 1,000: **If you had 100 ten-dollar bills, you would have a *thousand* dollars.** [33]

tie [tī] *v.* **1.** to fasten with a bow or knot: **Lupe's little brother just learned to *tie* his shoelaces. 2.** to have the same score in a game; be even: **Our team is losing by one run, so if we score again we'll *tie* the game.** —*n.* an even score in a game: **The game ended in a *tie* because each team had scored four goals.** [3]

tight [tīt] *adv.* firmly; not loosely: **Dad yelled, "Hold on *tight*!" when I started down the hill on my sled.** [3]

ti•tle [tī′təl] *n.* a championship: **Muhammad Ali won the boxing *title* of heavyweight champion of the world.** [29]

to•geth•er [tə·ge′thər] *adv.* mixed with or in contact with one another: **Let's all sit *together* at the same table.** [17, 32]

to•tal [tō′təl] *adj.* making up all of a thing; being the entire thing: **She added up the prices of our groceries and then gave us the *total* bill.** [33]

towns•folk [tounz′fōk′] *n.* people who live in a particular town: **Stores, schools, and offices were closed while the *townsfolk* watched the parade.** [3]

trek [trek] *n.* a long, difficult journey: **They survived stampedes and rattlesnakes in their *trek* across country.** [30] ◆

◆ **Trek** comes from the language of a people of southern Africa known as the Boers or Afrikaners. In the year 1836, some of these people made a long and difficult trip into new lands in Africa. This journey became known as the Great Trek. *Trek* was the word in their language for a trip in a wagon pulled by oxen. Since then the word *trek* has come to mean "a long, hard trip over rough ground."

trem•ble [trem′bəl] *v.*, **trembling, trembled.** to shake or shiver without control: **Tess began *trembling* with fear when the door to the lions' cage swung open.** [9]

truck [truk] *n.* a motor vehicle that is larger than a car and made to carry heavy loads: **Dad rented a *truck* to move our furniture to our new house.** [2]

try [trī] *n.*, **tries.** a single effort to do something: **After losing on two *tries* last week, I finally won a race.** [25]

tur•key [tûr′kē] *n.* a large reddish brown bird with a fan-shaped tail and a long neck: **Roasted *turkey* and pumpkin pie are my favorite Thanksgiving foods.** [28] ◆

◆ **Turkey** is the name of a large country between Europe and Asia. It is strange that the *turkey* is named for this country, because the bird does not live there. The early pioneers in America confused the turkey with another bird that was found in Turkey. The turkey is strictly an American bird. In fact, the patriot Benjamin Franklin wanted to make the turkey our national bird instead of the eagle.

turn [tûrn] *v.* to go in a certain direction: ***Turn* left at the stop sign.** [19]

a	add	ō	open	th	thin
ā	ace	ô	order	th	this
â	care	oi	oil	zh	vision
ä	palm	o͝o	took		
e	end	o͞o	pool	ə	**a** in about
ē	equal	ou	out		**e** in listen
i	it	u	up		**i** in pencil
ī	ice	û(r)	burn		**o** in melon
o	odd	yo͞o	use		**u** in circus

U

use•ful [yo͞os′fəl] *adj.* having a good use; being of use: **A flashlight is *useful* when you need to see in the dark.** *syn.* helpful [27]

V

veg•e•ta•tion [ve′jə·tā′shən] *n.* plant life: ***Vegetation* is thick around the river, where plants have enough water to grow.** [23]

ver•y [ver′ē] *adv.* to a high degree; more than usual: **Dave ate two hamburgers because he was *very* hungry.** [28]

vil•lage [vi′lij] *n.* a group of houses and other buildings that form a community smaller than a town: **Will would rather live in his small *village* than in a big city like New York.** [3, 26]

viv•id [vi′vəd] *adj.* bright and strong color or light: **Bright red is a more *vivid* color than pale gray.** [5]

W

wag [wag] *v.,* **wagging, wagged.** to move back and forth or up and down: **My dog shows that he's glad to see me by *wagging* his tail.** [20]

wag•on [wa′gən] *n.* a low vehicle with four wheels that is pulled by hand: **Jaleel fixed the wheel on his red *wagon*.** [34]

walk [wôk] *v.* to move on foot at a normal rate: **I can *walk* home from school because I live two blocks away.** —*n.* the act of walking, especially for pleasure or exercise: **I take my poodle for a *walk* every evening.** [10]

war [wôr] *n.* a long fight between countries or groups within a country: **This civil *war* is between groups of people within the same country.** [15]

warm [wôrm] *adj.* not too cold; somewhat hot: **Mom will keep our dinner *warm* on the stove.** [15]

wash [wosh] *v.* to get rid of dirt or stains with water or with soap and water: **Mom always tells me to *wash* my hands before we eat dinner.** [8]

wa•ter [wô′tər *or* wo′tər] *n.* the common liquid that falls from the sky as rain and forms the oceans, lakes, and rivers: **The Pacific Ocean is a very large body of *water*.** [32]

way [wā] *n.* a certain method to do or get something: **Please show us the *way* you trained your dog to do tricks.** [4]

wear [wâr] *v.* to have on the body: **Mom said to *wear* old clothes when I help Dad paint the fence.** [14]

went [went] *v.* the past form of *go*: **We took our beach ball along when we *went* swimming.** [1]

we've [wēv] *cont.* a short form for *we have*: **We will make some lemonade if *we've* got enough lemons.** [22]

what's [(h)wuts] *cont.* a short form for *what is* or *what has*: ***What's* the answer to your riddle? *What's* happened to the book I left on this chair?** [22]

wheat [wēt *or* hwēt] *n.* a tall grass plant with long leaves on a thin stem used as a grain for food: **Grandpa said people make bread out of the *wheat* he grows on his farm.** [8]

wheat

where [wâr *or* hwâr] *adv.* at or in what place: **I know *where* I'll hide when we play hide-and-seek.** [8]

whine [wīn *or* hwīn] *v.,* **whining, whined.** to cry in a complaining way: **Diane's dog barked and *whined* when we made him stay outside during the party.** [8]

white [wīt *or* hwīt] *adj.* having the lightest of all colors: **The *white* snow stuck to our faces during the snowball fight.** [3]

whoop [h(w)o͞op *or* h(w)o͝op] *v.* to make a loud cry or shout: **Our team *whooped* with joy when we won the game.** [8]

wildlife

wild•life [wīld´līf´] *n.* animals and plants that live naturally in a wild area: **You can see** *wildlife* **best at dawn or at dusk, the times many animals feed.** [23] ◆

> ◆ **Wildlife** means "animals, such as wolves or deer, that live on their own in nature." Not all animals live this way. Some animals, such as dogs and cats, are kept by people as pets. Others, such as cows and horses, are raised by people for food or used to do work. The word *wildlife* does not apply to these animals.

wind•y [win´dē] *adj.* having much wind: **When I see the flag flapping, I know it's** *windy* **outside.** [30]

win•ter [win´tər] *n.* the season after fall and before spring: *Winter* **is Karen's favorite season because she loves snow.** [17]

won [wun] *v.* came in first; took first place: **Our team** *won* **the game because we scored more points.** [16]

wood [wood] *n.* the hard material that makes up the trunk and branches of a tree or bush: **Dad and I chopped** *wood* **to burn in our fireplace.** [9]

word [wûrd] *n.* the smallest part of a language that has a meaning when used alone: **You can look up the meaning of a** *word* **in your dictionary.** [19]

wore [wôr] *v.* the past form of *wear;* had on the body; put on the body: **Ellen** *wore* **shorts to the picnic because the weather was warm.** [15]

work [wûrk] *n.* what a person does to earn money; a job: **Dad goes to** *work* **at his office every weekday.** —*v.* to use one's body or mind to do something: **If we all** *work* **together, we'll finish the job faster.** [19]

work•sheet [wûrk´shēt´] *n.* a paper used for school studies that has spaces for the student to write in: **First fill out your** *worksheet,* **and then check for spelling mistakes.** [28]

write [rīt] *v.,* writing, wrote, written. **1.** to form letters or words on paper or another such surface: **We have to** *write* **our names on the upper right-hand corner of the paper. 2.** to use words to make a book, article, or other work: **I'll** *write* **my letter and then take it to the post office. Mom asked if I had** *written* **Aunt Liz a thank-you note for my present. Ben** *wrote* **his book report the night before it was due.** [7, 26]

wrong [rông] *adj.* not as it should be; not correct: **I was** *wrong* **when I said, "Two plus two equals five."** *syn.* incorrect [7]

wrote *v.* the past form of *write.* [7]

Y

yard [yärd] *n.* an area of open land around a house or other building: **We play games in the** *yard* **at recess.** [14]

year [yēr] *n.* a period of time that is made up of 365 days (or in a leap year, 366 days), beginning on January 1 and ending on December 31: **Are you having a birthday party this** *year*? [17]

yel•low [ye´lō] *adj.* having the color of butter or ripe lemons: **The yolk of an egg is** *yellow.* [26]

your [yôr *or* yoor] *poss. pron.* of or belonging to you: *Your* **twin looks just like you.** [15]

Z

zoo [zoō] *n.* a special park or other place where wild animals are kept for people to see: **Dad warned me not to stand too close to the animals' cages at the** *zoo.* [9]

a	add	ō	open	th	thin
ā	ace	ô	order	th	this
â	care	oi	oil	zh	vision
ä	palm	oo	took		
e	end	ōo	pool	ə	**a** in about
ē	equal	ou	out		**e** in listen
i	it	u	up		**i** in pencil
ī	ice	û(r)	burn		**o** in melon
o	odd	yoo	use		**u** in circus

The Writing Process

WHEN WRITING, you can use a plan called the writing process to help you think of ideas and then write about them. The writing process has five stages. You can work on your writing in different ways by moving back and forth through the stages. The following are descriptions of the stages.

PREWRITING
Identify your task, audience, and purpose for writing. Then choose a topic. Gather and organize information about the topic.

DRAFTING
Put your ideas in writing. Don't worry about making mistakes. You can fix them later.

PREWRITING Sometimes you might find it difficult to think of a topic. Ideas for topics can come from many places. Topics can be something you already know or would like to know more about, something you've read, or something that has happened to you.

You can organize your ideas in several ways. You might use a list, an outline, a story map, a web, or a drawing.

DRAFTING When you put your ideas on paper, use your organizer to help you use the correct order. If you make a mistake, keep writing. You can go back to fix it later.

Remember that once you finish each stage of the writing process, you can return to a previous stage or go on to the next stage.

If you're not happy with what you've written, start over.

PROOFREADING Once you have finished making changes, you are ready to fix your mistakes. Use editors' marks to fix mistakes and make changes. Use the Proofreading Checklist to help you.

PUBLISHING Here are some ideas you can use to publish your work.
- Read it aloud.
- Turn it into a play or a Readers Theatre.
- Print it on a computer.
- Make an audiotape or a videotape.
- Illustrate your story, and show your audience the pictures as they listen to you read.

▶ **RESPONDING AND REVISING**
Reread your writing to see whether it meets your purpose. Meet with a partner or group to discuss and revise your writing.

▶ **PROOFREADING**
Correct any spelling, grammar, usage, mechanics, and capitalization errors.

▶ **PUBLISHING**
Share your writing. Decide how you want to publish your work.

Proofreading Checklist
- ✓ Circle any words you are not sure you have spelled correctly. Then look them up in a dictionary, or ask for help from someone who knows how to spell them.
- ✓ Look for words you have misspelled before. Add them to your Spelling Log.
- ✓ If you are not sure how to spell a word, try saying it slowly. Listen to every syllable. Have you written all the syllables?
- ✓ Make sure you have indented each paragraph.
- ✓ Check your capitalization and punctuation.
- ✓ Do you want to take out something or add something?

RESPONDING AND REVISING When you read your own or someone else's writing, look for the following: a good beginning and ending, clear words, and details that relate to the topic.

When someone makes suggestions about your writing, you can decide whether or not to make those changes.

Integrated Spelling   THE WRITING PROCESS

Spelling Strategies

Let us show you some of our favorite spelling strategies!

Here's a tip that helps me spell a word. I **say** the word. Then I **picture** the way it is spelled. Then I **write** it!

When I'm learning how to spell a word, the **Study Steps to Learn a Word** are a big help. See pages 8 and 9.

I think of ways to spell the vowel sounds in a word. Then I **try different spellings** until the word looks right.

When I don't know how to spell a word, I sometimes just take my best **guess!** Then I **check** it.

Sometimes I **read** the sentences **backward.** I start with the last word and end with the first word. It really helps me notice words I've misspelled! Then I proofread for meaning.

I **proofread** my work **twice.** First, I circle words I know are misspelled. Then, I look for words I'm not sure of.

I look for **homophones** and make sure each word I've written makes sense.

When I'm writing a **compound word,** I think about how the **two smaller words** are spelled.

If I'm not sure how to spell a word correctly, I take a **guess.** Then I look up the word in a **dictionary.**

Sometimes thinking of a **rhyming word** helps me figure out how to spell a word.

I think about **spelling rules** like how to change the spelling before adding *-ed* or *-ing*.

Drawing the **shape** of a word helps me remember its spelling. This is the shape of the word .

When I **proofread,** I like to **work with a partner.** First, I read the words aloud as my partner looks at the spelling. Then we switch jobs.

My Spelling Log

WHAT'S A SPELLING LOG? It's a special place where you can keep track of words that are important to you. Just look at what you'll find in your Spelling Log!

Spelling Words to Study

This is a great place for you to list the words you need to study. There is a column for each unit of your spelling book.

Vocabulary WordShop Words

Every spelling lesson has a list of words on the Vocabulary WordShop page. List them where you think they belong. There are special pages for...

Language Words...page 186
Social Studies and Science Words...page 187
Art and Music Words...page 188.

My Own Word Collection

Be a word collector, and keep your collection here! Sort words you want to remember into fun categories you make up yourself!

Spelling Words to Study

List the words from each lesson that need your special attention. Be sure to list the words you misspelled on the Pretest.

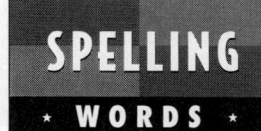

UNIT 1	UNIT 2
Lesson 1	Lesson 7
Lesson 2	Lesson 8
Lesson 3	Lesson 9
Lesson 4	Lesson 10
Lesson 5	Lesson 11

Spelling Words to Study

UNIT 3	UNIT 4
Lesson 13	Lesson 19
Lesson 14	Lesson 20
Lesson 15	Lesson 21
Lesson 16	Lesson 22
Lesson 17	Lesson 23

Spelling Words to Study

UNIT 5	UNIT 6
Lesson 25	Lesson 32
Lesson 26	Lesson 33
Lesson 27	Lesson 34
Lesson 28	Lesson 35
Lesson 29	
Lesson 30	

Integrated Spelling

WordShop
WORDS

Language Words

These pages are for listing Vocabulary WordShop Words. Group words that you think go together in a category. The words themselves may give you ideas about ways to group them. Use ideas of your own, too!

Add a clue beside a word to help you remember it. The clue might be a picture, a sentence, a definition, or just a note.

Compound Words

Rhyming Words

Funny Words

- *i* Before *e* Words
- Double-Letter Words
- Words from Other Languages
- Very Amazing Adverbs
- Sound Words
- Soft Words

Social Studies and Science Words

Put Social Studies and Science Words into groups on this page.

Cloud Words

Communication Words

Places

Country Words
Factory Words
Money Words
History Words
Farm Words
River Words

Integrated Spelling

VOCABULARY WORDSHOP WORDS 187

WordShop WORDS

Art and Music Words

This page is for Art and Music Words!

Rhythmic Words

Musical Words

Art Supply Words

Color Words
Words About Shapes
Names of Instruments
Painting Words
Favorite-Song Words
Piano Words
Woodworking Words

My Own Word Collection

When you read and listen, be on the lookout for words you want to remember. Group them into categories any way you like, and write them on these pages. Pretty soon you'll have a word collection of your very own!

Unusual Words

Spooky Words

Words That Rhyme with My Name

Cheerful Words

Awesome Words

Integrated Spelling

Your Own WORDS

My Own Word Collection

Save words you really like in your collection. Include words you have trouble pronouncing or spelling.

Hard-to-Say Words
Words About Friends
Messy Words
Words That Describe
Hard-to-Group Words

My Own Word Collection

Think of different ways to sort the words in your collection!
Collecting words can be so much fun!

Strange Words
Classroom Words
Dry Words
Quiet Words
Compound Words

My Own Word Collection

List some of your favorite words.

Words That Sound Funny
Rainy-Day Words
Vacation Words
Game Words
Ice-Cream Words